Music in Mexico

Music in Mexico

∞

EXPERIENCING MUSIC, EXPRESSING CULTURE

∞

ALEJANDRO L. MADRID

OXFORD
UNIVERSITY PRESS

Oxford University Press is a department of the University of Oxford. It furthers the University's objective of excellence in research, scholarship, and education by publishing worldwide.

Oxford   New York
Auckland   Cape Town   Dar es Salaam   Hong Kong   Karachi
Kuala Lumpur   Madrid   Melbourne   Mexico City   Nairobi
New Delhi   Shanghai   Taipei   Toronto

With offices in
Argentina   Austria   Brazil   Chile   Czech Republic   France   Greece
Guatemala   Hungary   Italy   Japan   Poland   Portugal   Singapore
South Korea   Switzerland   Thailand   Turkey   Ukraine   Vietnam

For titles covered by Section 112 of the US Higher Education Opportunity Act, please visit www.oup.com/us/he for the latest information about pricing and alternate formats.

Published by Oxford University Press.
198 Madison Avenue, New York, NY 10016
www.oup.com

Oxford is a registered trademark of Oxford University Press

Library of Congress Cataloging-in-Publication Data

Madrid-González, Alejandro L. (Alejandro Luis)
   Music in Mexico : experiencing music, expressing culture / by Alejandro L. Madrid.—1st ed.
       p. cm.—(Global music series)
   Includes bibliographical references and index.
   ISBN 978-0-19-981280-6
   1. Popular music-Mexico—History and criticism.   I. Title.
ML3485.M34 2013
780.92—dc23   2012043251

Printing number: 9 8 7 6

Printed in the United States of America
on acid-free paper

GLOBAL MUSIC SERIES

General Editors: Bonnie C. Wade and Patricia Shehan Campbell

Music in East Africa, Gregory Barz
Music in Turkey, Eliot Bates
Music in Central Java, Benjamin Brinner
Teaching Music Globally, Patricia Shehan Campbell
Music in Portugal and Spain, Salwa El-Shawan Castelo-Branco
and Susan Moreno Fernández
Native American Music in Eastern North America, Beverley Diamond
Music in Pacific Island Cultures, Brian Diettrich, Jane Freeman Moulin,
and Michael Webb
Music in Mainland Southeast Asia, Gavin Douglas
Carnival Music in Trinidad, Shannon Dudley
Music in Bali, Lisa Gold
Music in Ireland, Dorothea E. Hast and Stanley Scott
Music in Korea, Donna Lee Kwon
Music in China, Frederick Lau
Music in Mexico, Alejandro Madrid
Music in Egypt, Scott Marcus
Music in the Hispanic Caribbean, Robin Moore
Music in Brazil, John Patrick Murphy
Intertribal Native American Music in the United States, John-Carlos Perea
Music in America, Adelaide Reyes
Music in Bulgaria, Timothy Rice
Music in North India, George Ruckert
Mariachi Music in America, Daniel Sheehy
Music in West Africa, Ruth M. Stone
Music in the Andes, Thomas Turino
Music in South India, T. Viswanathan and Matthew Harp Allen
Music in Japan, Bonnie C. Wade
Thinking Musically, Bonnie C. Wade

Contents

∞

Preface

∞

When I was invited to write this brief volume about music in Mexico I was hesitant about accepting for two reasons. One, most of my scholarship deals with transnational flows and postnational interpretative frameworks; thus writing a book about music in a very localized geographic location seemed a contradiction. Second, I have also been very critical of musical canons and was not particularly excited about writing a book that dealt with Mexican canonic musical practices or with the prospect of creating a new canon of Mexican music. Regardless of these reservations, I accepted the invitation as a I saw it as an opportunity to further my belief that we need to move away from the nation-state as a unit of interpretation as well as a chance to question stereotypes of Mexican music. Thus, I set out to write a book about the musics that Mexicans grow up listening to in their everyday life and how these practices are informed by continual histories of migration and transnational flows. Since it is impossible to cover all of Mexico's diverse musical traditions in this textbook I focus on a selection of contemporary music practices that have remained neglected in the sonic representation of Mexican culture both in Mexico and abroad.

I have excluded some musical forms that have become stereotypes of Mexicanness in the country and abroad. My intention is not to say they are meaningless musical practices, since clearly they are not. Instead, I challenge the representations about Mexican culture that these genres have helped reproduce, focusing on contemporary musical practices that Mexicans grow up listening to such as *norteña, banda, bolero, balada,* and forms of alternative music like rock and *canto nuevo*. While mariachi and other *sones* and folk musics are heard by Mexicans on special occasions and celebrations, they do not really form part of their everyday musical experience. This means I do not focus on folk musics because with rare exceptions, they are not what most Mexicans favor as part of their daily social interactions or what surrounds them growing up. Moreover, many of the folk musics that have become symbols of Mexico through government-sponsored institutions such as the Ballet Folklórico de México (Mexico's Folk Ballet Company) are stylized, re-choreographed, and re-contextualized exhibition practices that do not really exist as such among regular folks in urban areas or the countryside. There, one is more likely to hear local variants of *norteña, banda, cumbia, balada,* rock, as well as local folk traditions that have continued independent of those government-sponsored practices—but being local, these traditions do not represent the larger musical experience of most Mexicans. *Banda, norteña, bolero, balada,* and rock are the genres and styles that sell millions of records in the Americas and receive Grammy Awards every year. These are the musics Americans are more likely to hear in Mexico or in the houses of their Mexican or Mexican American friends in the United States; they truly reflect the contemporary experience of Mexicans and speak to the many social issues affecting Mexico. Finally, although I briefly mention mariachi in relation to *son* traditions like *son jarocho* and *bolero ranchero,* I have not included a larger discussion of this practice mainly because Daniel Sheehy's book in this series provides a lengthy, in-depth discussion of this music tradition.

Mainstream representations of Mexican culture in the United States developed in terms of Otherness as necessary for the construction of a U.S. identity. Central to any construction of identity is the notion of difference. Identity is defined by what one is not as much as by what one is or aspires to be; thus, claims to individual and collective identity always need to recognize those who are different from us in order to develop a sense of our community and ourselves. Constructions of national identity are not different; in order to define the nation and its residents it is fundamental to define those who do not belong in it. For historical and cultural reasons, Mexico and Mexicans have figured prominently as that Other when shaping the discourse of U.S. differentiation. The United States, in order to be defined as a prosperous, civilized, law-abiding, largely white, Protestant, hard-working, English speaking nation, had to be contrasted with a representative of the opposite of those ideals; thus, Mexico and Mexicans came to embody poorness, barbarism, criminality, non-whiteness (or indigeneity), Catholicism, indolence, and unsophisticatedness. In the U.S. imagination Mexico became the quintessential Other; a representation continuously reinforced by a history of military, political, and economic conflict between the two nations. Such discourse also validated the 19th-century U.S. expansionist project, and was used as a symbolic excuse to conquer the Mexican territory that became the American Southwest. That a large majority of contemporary Mexican working migrants come from poor indigenous and mestizo communities forced to cross the border without documents by economic and political systems that marginalize and discriminate against them in both countries has helped reinforce these misguided representations. However, the musics Mexicans grow up listening to, which are the result of lengthy processes of globalization, indicate that their dreams and aspirations are no different from those of Americans. One goal of this book is to show United States students that regardless of obvious cultural and ethnic differences, there are many points of contact and similarities between U.S. and Mexican peoples.

Music in Mexico is divided into seven chapters. Chapter 1 introduces the three overarching themes of the book: (1) "Mexico's troubled legacy with its indigenous past has shaped the representation of the country and its culture"; (2) "Most musical genres in contemporary Mexico are the result of migration"; and (3) "The TV, radio, and film industries of Mexico have played a powerful role in the development of a sense of Mexican music within Mexico and abroad." The themes are presented in such a way as to provide the student with a basic knowledge of Mexico's history in order to inform contemporary musical practices. Chapter 2 examines the renaissance of *son jarocho* in contemporary Mexico and its embrace by Mexican American communities. Chapters 3 and 4 focus on the Mexican romantic song complex, especially its two most popular genres, the *bolero* and the *balada*. In Chapter 3, the *bolero* is taken in order to show cultural connections between Mexico and the Caribbean and to study the construction of traditional gender roles in Mexico. Chapter 4 takes the *balada* as a case study to explore the powerful role of Mexican media in shaping musical tastes throughout Latin America as well as ways in which mainstream musicians may challenge traditional gender constructions. Chapters 5 and 6 deconstruct the idea of "Regional Mexican Music," an umbrella label used to market a wide variety of heterogenous Mexican musical traditions, especially *norteña* and *banda* musics. By examining *norteña* and *banda* musics in relation to the Mexican diaspora, these chapters show the importance of Mexican migrant communities in shaping contemporary Mexican musical culture. Chapter 7 discusses underground musical practices like rock and *canto nuevo* in order to show different ways in which the development of Mexican music has responded to a variety of social concerns and cultural practices that transcend the boundaries of the country.

ACKNOWLEDGMENTS

This book would not have been possible without the enthusiasm, commitment, guidance, and passion of many people. I would like to thank my colleagues from the Latin American and Caribbean Music section of the Society for Ethnomusicology, especially Raquel Paraíso and Randall Ch. Kohl for providing information and materials about *son jarocho*. I am indebted to Ricardo Pérez Montfort, Victor Pichardo, Julia del Palacio, Raul Fernandez, Gina Gamboa, Maya Zazhil Fernandez, and Micaela Díaz-Sánchez for sharing with me their work and experiences as *son jarocho* musicians and researchers. My appreciation goes to Tom Keller, Matanya Ophee, Fred Maus, and Alejandro Moreno Villarreal for their insight regarding double string instruments, and to Fritz Torres for sharing with me anecdotes about many *balada* singers. Sincere thanks to my dear friend Ernesto Cuevas for sharing his passion for romantic and pop Mexican music with me. (Who would have thought that after decades of musical differences but unflagging friendship it would be the *balada* that would bring us musically together?) I am particularly thankful to all of those who followed my Facebook updates as this book was taking shape; there are too many to name them all, but I would like to acknowledge that their feedback and encouragement were very important in clarifying important issues to be discussed and in keeping me going when the task became too tiresome.

Thanks are due to Eloy Cruz, Dan Sheehy, Mary Farquharson, Juan Sebastián Lach, David Filio, and Carlos Porcel de Peralta for granting permissions for the use of the music tracks in the accompanying CD; as well as Ekaterina Pirozhenko, Nicole Guidotti-Hernandez, Angelos Quetzalcoatl, and Edwin González for their help locating or securing photographs for the book. Very special thanks to Bonnie Wade and Patricia Campbell who have read drafts of the manuscript and offered countless suggestions to improve it, and to Cameron Quevedo for working on the book's instructional manual. I am also deeply indebted to the anonymous readers of the manuscript whose suggestions and advice were always illuminating. Finally, thanks to the staff at Oxford University Press: Janet Beatty, Lauren Mine, Nichole LeFebvre, Sheena Kowalski, Marianne Paul, and Richard Carlin; their hard work and commitment have made my own work much easier.

CD Track List

∞

1. "La María Chuchena." Recorded by Santana Alonso Vidal (*requinto* and lead vocalist), Severiano Chipol Xolo (*requinto*), and Emiliano Toto Urbano (*jarana tercera*) in San Andrés Tuxtla, Veracruz, Mexico, on May 6, 1976. From *Antología del son de México*. 1985. Discos Corasón CO 102. 2002.

2. "La Jota" / "La María Chuchena." Ensamble Continuo. From *Laberinto en la guitarra. El espíritu barroco del son jarocho*. 2004. Urtext UMA 2018. 2004.

3. Guty Cárdenas and Luis Rosado Vega, "Pasión." Guty Cárdenas. From *Guty Cárdenas. Un siglo del ruiseñor*. Discos Corasón COV 201. 2006.

4. Agustín Lara, "Aventurera." Los Tres Reyes. From *Romancing the Past*. Smithsonian Folkways Recordings SFW 40562. 2011.

5. "Máquina 501." Antonio Federico, Hipólito Romero, Frank Moreno, and Paul Romero. From *Heroes and Horses: Corridos from the Arizona-Sonora Borderlands*. Smithsonian Folkways Recordings SFW 40475. 2002.

6. Severiano Briseño, "El sinaloense." Banda Los Guamuchileños. From *Bandas Sinaloenses. "Música Tambora."* Arhoolie Folklyric CD 7048. 2001. Available from www.arhoolie.com.

7. Santa Sabina and Xavier Villaurrutia, "Canción." Santa Sabina. From *Mar adentro en la sangre*. Discos Babel. 2000.

8. Carlos Porcel de Peralta "Nahuel," "Vienen cantando." Mexicanto. From *Coincidir*. Discos Pueblo CDDP 1432. 2009.

Music in Mexico

CHAPTER 1

Introduction

On April 30, 2010, Chicago's House of Blues became a niche of Mexican musical culture as a great crowd, primarily Mexicans and Mexican Americans, gathered to fervently applaud and sing along with Lila Downs. Lila appeared, wearing high-heeled tall boots, a waistband over-knee skirt, a tube top beautifully decorated with Oaxaca-style embroidery, and a white shawl resembling the wings of a sparrow, to passionately sing Tomás Méndez's classic *ranchera* song "Cucurrucucú paloma" (Coo Coo Dove); it was clear then that this was going to be an extraordinary evening. The crowd, mesmerized, almost hypnotized by Lila's beautiful, expressive voice, enjoyed her rendition of *rancheras*, *huapangos*, *boleros*, *corridos*, and *sones*, including "Arenita azul" (Blue Little Sand), with a powerful percussive beat that invited everyone to dance. Her soulful versions, in Spanish, Zapotec, Mixtec, and Nahuatl languages, of classic Oaxacan songs like "La llorona" (The Weeping Woman), "La zandunga," and "Simuna" (Simona) brought nostalgic tears to the many Oaxaqueños (from Oaxaca state in Southern Mexico) in the audience. However, her wonderful medley of Woody Guthrie's classics "Pastures of Plenty" and "This Land Is Your Land," reinvented with *cumbia* and hip-hop touches, brought down the house, the crowd screaming and singing, accompanying Lila's performance.

Lila Downs's concert at the House of Blues was no ordinary performance. Occurring in Chicago, with its large Mexican and Mexican American communities, during the heated national debate about immigration and Arizona's SB 1070 law; Lila's "Mexicanized" renditions of Guthrie's classic odes to the working classes strongly resonated with this audience. Guthrie's "Pastures of Plenty" (1941) chronicles the experience of migrant workers going to California and Arizona to harvest crops while living "on the cities' edges." In the present anti-immigration context, Downs's appropriation of the song was a statement of how Mexican migrants and Mexican American workers embody the powerful tale that connects U.S. identity to immigration, hard work, and determination.

I also think that Downs' concert reflects the ways in which the wonderful kaleidoscope of contemporary Mexican culture is developed in complex dialogues that transcend Mexico's political borders. Lila's singing in multiple languages spoke to the multi-ethnic character of Mexico, for it is home to more than 60 indigenous ethnic groups with their own languages. And her engaging interpretation of "Arenita azul," a traditional *chilena* from the Costa Chica region in Oaxaca and Guerrero, reminds us of Mexico's forgotten Afro-Mexican population. The African presence, dating to the 16th century when it numbered roughly a half-million, was neglected during the re-imagings of the Mexican nation even though smaller groups of Africans, Afro-Caribbeans, and African Americans kept migrating to Mexico until the end of the 19th and sometimes through the 20th century. Mexico's European heritage is also diverse, and although most Europeans arrived from Spain during colonial times, many ethnicities and cultures have immigrated through Mexico's history, including Germans, Italians, French, as well as Chinese, Japanese, Jews, and Arabs. Figure 1.1 offers a map of Mexico that shows the location of the main cities and cultural areas discussed in the book.

1. Tijuana–San Diego, California
2. Ciudad Juárez–El Paso, Texas
3. Monterrey
4. Reynosa–McAllen, Texas
5. Culiacán
6. Mazatlán
7. Durango
8. Zacatecas
9. Guadalajara
10. Mexico City
11. Veracruz
12. Acapulco
13. Oaxaca
14. Progreso
15. Mérida
16. Sotavento region
17. Los Angeles, California
18. Tucson, Arizona
19. San Antonio, Texas

FIGURE 1.1.   *Map of Mexico.*

Lila's repertory—traditional genres, jazz, and hip-hop—speaks to the wide variety of experiences and aspirations of Mexico's people. The history of some of these songs shows how powerful media shaped symbols of Mexican music and popular culture and its representation throughout the world. In the 1965 film *Cucurrucucú paloma*, singer Lola Beltrán introduced the song "Cucurrucucú paloma," and with the help of Latin America's influential radio and TV networks, XEW and Televisa, made it and herself into icons of Mexican *ranchera* and mariachi music.

The three issues I have mentioned in relation to Lila Downs' concert in Chicago—ethnicity and the place of indigeneity among symbols of Mexican identity, the role of migration and diaspora in determining Mexican culture, and the power of the media in shaping its national and international representations—are the central themes for discussion of Mexican music in this book. Figure 1.2 shows Lila Downs performing at Chicago's Congress Theater.

FIGURE 1.2.   *Lila Downs performing at Chicago's Congress Theater.* (© *Oliver Gillinson. Used by permission of Oliver Gillinson, 2012)*

ETHNIC IDENTITY AND MUSIC IN MEXICO

Lila Downs was born in Tlaxiaco, Oaxaca, the daughter of a Scottish American father and a Mixtec Indian mother. She grew up a multicultural child traveling back and forth between Mexico and the United States and negotiating the intricacies of crossing the borders between mainstream Mexican and indigenous cultures. Lila experienced both the benefits of living in many cultures and the shortcomings of not being fully accepted in any of them; to mainstream Mexicans she was an Indian, to Americans she was Mexican, and to indigenous Oaxacans she was *mestizo* (person of mixed ancestry) or just American. As a member of Mixtec and Trique communities she experienced the discrimination and disrespect suffered by indigenous people in Mexico. Her choice of songs and language celebrate the many cultures she claims as her own and substantiates the many hardships that come with crossing borders.

The mainstream American belief that links Mexicans and their culture to indigeneity is not only the result of American constructions of difference but is also a response to Mexico's conflicted relationship with its own indigenous population. The country celebrates such a population in textbooks but neglects it in everyday life. Throughout Mexican history numerous political projects have attempted to use indigenous cultures as banners of Mexican identity. The first theme I use to explore music in Mexico concerns the relationship between music and different constructions of ethnic identity in the country. Formulated simply, Mexico's troubled legacy with its indigenous past has shaped the representation of the country and its culture.

Although interest in indigenous communities among Mexican intellectuals persisted from the late 19th century, it was after the Mexican revolution (1910–21), particularly during the administration of President Lázaro Cárdenas in the 1930s, that a political project called *indigenismo* attempted to make indigenous cultures the source of a unified Mexican identity. This project encouraged artists to base their contemporary art on pre-Columbian forms, images, and sounds. For plastic artists this was not problematic given that pre-Columbian paintings, architecture, and ceramics, still survive and could be taken as models. It proved more difficult for musicians since most indigenous musical practices in Mexico are strongly influenced by European (mostly Spanish) and African musics. As scholars like Marina Alonso Bolaños argue, indigenous music had to be imagined and invented both in the modernist concert music of composers like Manuel M. Ponce, Carlos Chávez, or Daniel Ayala and in the stylized versions of folk musics produced by state-sponsored organizations like the Departamento de Bellas Artes (Fine Arts Department) or the Ballet Folklórico de México (Alonso Bolaños 2008). The stylistic character, social role, instrumental lineup, and even repertory of most current musical practices in rural Mexico were determined by how the *indigenista* project reconstructed them to make them symbols of the heritage of the nation-state. This official celebration of indigeneity was defined in relation to the political goals of the nation but was accompanied by a striking neglect, marginalization, and contempt toward indigenous peoples and their living culture. As a result of these policies, today there are two contrasting and co-existing notions of indigeneity in Mexico: an imaginary one, in which being indigenous is a source of pride in the splendor of pre-Columbian civilizations, and the real one that identifies contemporary indigenous people and their culture as "backward," marginal, and a source of embarrassment.

Through the 20th century, *indigenismo* shared the spotlight in Mexican cultural politics with an idea of *mestizaje* (racial and cultural mixing) that privileges the mixing of European and indigenous cultures as the root of Mexican identity. This notion of *mestizaje* as a celebratory concept was loosely based on the spirit of José Vasconcelos's renowned *La raza cósmica* (1925). In his book, Vasconcelos advanced the idea that Hispanic America's *raza de bronce* (bronze race; a combination of all the world's races and cultures mixing in the continent) had the spiritual mission of establishing a true universal and cosmopolitan civilization. As a national cultural project, *mestizaje* lost its cosmopolitan basis and the catholicity of Vasconcelos's ideas and focused on the claim that Mexico's local *raza de bronce* resulted only from Spanish and indigenous mixing. Despite the shift from indigenous to *mestizo* culture, indigeneity remained a central theme in the national discourse of *mestizaje* and the new mestizo nation's claims to authenticity as it established an apparent difference between Mexico and other North American and Caribbean nations and laid the "moral" claim to lands of pre-Columbian civilizations for the Mexican nation-state.

Although this construction of identity authenticated Mexico as a unique mestizo nation due to its strong "roots" in an indigenous pre-Columbian past, it also helped render invisible the country's black heritage, as Africa had no place in this dichotomous understanding of national identity. As a result, *indigenismo* and *mestizaje* as cultural politics reduced blackness in Mexico to sporadic and isolated moments in the country's history. The power and influence of these ideologies was such that even today one often hears Mexicans saying that "there are no blacks in Mexico" and explaining instances of blackness as coming from the Caribbean, particularly Cuba.

The study of indigenous musics falls outside the focus of this book, although the contradictions in Mexico's idea of indigeneity are certainly of concern to us. Examining these contradictions offers a chance to understand numerous traditional folk and popular musics and the meaning of their continuity or revival both in contemporary Mexico and among Mexican Americans. This theme allows for a study of the racial and ethnic tensions surrounding the production, consumption, circulation, and regulation of music and music-related practices.

MUSIC, MIGRATION, AND DIASPORA IN MEXICO

Lila Downs's Chicago House of Blues concert indicates the importance of migration in contemporary Mexican culture. Her appropriation and transformation of Woody Guthrie's songs into symbols of the Mexican and Mexican American migratory experience show how music crosses cultural and geographic borders, becoming meaningful for people who live in conditions very different from those of the ones who produced it. This is one of the powers of music; it has the ability to be adopted, adapted, transformed, and made meaningful in various individual and collective spaces, histories, and circumstances. If specific songs are transformed through these cultural crossings, migrating musical genres also become something different as they cross borders and encounter different realities. The migration and diaspora of people and their cultures are fundamental in the creation of musical traditions. Paying attention to these forces is the goal of the second theme I have chosen in this volume; expressed simply, most musical genres in contemporary Mexico are the result of migration.

This notion may be evident in genres recently popularized throughout Mexico but not so obvious for older practices considered traditionally Mexican. Indeed, the economic success of documented and undocumented working-class Mexican immigrants to the United States in the last 30 years has dramatically affected mainstream Mexican popular culture. Just as race and ethnicity are central to my first theme, class issues are essential to my second. Most undocumented Mexican emigrants come to the United States not to live on welfare but to work, and work very hard, helping the United States economy by investing, consuming goods and services, increasing productivity, paying taxes, and contributing to Social Security, Medicare, and other public services even though they cannot receive these benefits due to their migratory status.

These migrants are also essential to the Mexican economy. Between 2000 and 2003, remittances from Mexican emigrants ranged between 10% and 35% of the country's gross domestic product. The economic power of this once-neglected sector of Mexico's population also translates into cultural capital as their cultural taste has also been incorporated into the Mexican mainstream.

The continuous filtration into the country's media of the kinds of music preferred by these emigrants has radically changed the Mexican popular music landscape since the 1990s. The popularization of musical genres and practices like *banda*, *norteña*, *onda grupera*, and more recently *pasito duranguense*, which entered the country's mainstream media during that decade, is a transnational phenomenon by which we can examine class tensions that surround music making in Mexico. Furthermore, understanding the flow of these transnational contemporary phenomena as part of larger globalization processes also helps us appreciate traditional Mexican musics as the outcome of different types of historical migratory flows and exchanges.

If this somewhat recent emigration has been fundamental in redefining popular music in Mexico in the last 20 years, the country's long history of immigration has also played a major role in shaping traditional regional folk musics. The history of Mexico, its people, and its culture is one of transnational crossings, contacts, and transculturation since the 16th century. These diasporic flows brought together different traditions that developed the new cultural formations that we recognize as Mexican. The shaping of these cultural formations was not harmonious but resulted from numerous historical power struggles based on racial, ethnic, class, and epistemological differences; the dynamics of these uneven encounters are fundamental in understanding contemporary Mexican culture.

The term "transculturation" was coined by Cuban writer Fernando Ortiz in an attempt to explain that cultural encounters are complex processes; when cultures meet, they are changed and transformed into new hybrid forms. Music offers a unique venue for exploring these processes since musical style is a prime example of these cultural negotiations. The musical genres I discuss are perfect cases for understanding the transculturation they have undergone as they have traveled with immigrants to Mexico throughout its history, moving outside the country with the powerful Mexican entertainment industry or with Mexican migrants going back and forth between Mexico and the United States. It is precisely because they are the result of diasporic flows, migrations, contacts, and processes of transculturation that are articulated locally, that traditional Mexican musics are very important depositories of local cultural capital.

MEDIA AND MUSIC IN MEXICO

Earlier I described "Cucurucucú paloma" as one of the most famous songs of the *ranchera* music repertoire, and a very good example of the power of the Mexican media to shape and circulate musical culture within and outside the country. One could argue that *ranchera* music as we know it today, one of the musical styles most closely associated with the mariachi ensemble, is largely an invention of the Mexican film and radio industries, later solidified by Mexico's powerful TV industry. Great Mexican *ranchera* music singers, from Tito Guizar to Lola Beltrán, were also stars of *comedia ranchera* (ranch play, a Mexican film genre featuring *ranchera* music). Mid-century Mexico's film and radio industries were critical in the development of *ranchera* music and mariachi as symbols of the nation and vehicles for the popularization of singer/ actors. The third theme I have chosen to guide our exploration of music in Mexico takes this as a point of departure and can be expressed simply: the TV, radio, and film industries of Mexico have played a powerful role in developing a sense of Mexican music within Mexico and abroad.

Because Mexican culture is largely unknown or misrepresented in everyday U.S. life, most Americans are unaware of the power of Mexico's entertainment industry. Mexico is the largest music market in Latin America and the eighth largest in the world, testimony to the fundamental role of the media in shaping a culture of cosmopolitan aspirations nationally and internationally. In addition to its contemporary importance, historically the powerful Mexican entertainment industry has been instrumental in the dissemination of Mexican music and culture throughout Latin America, sometimes to the detriment of local music scenes and traditions. By heavily promoting and selling their popular culture through soap operas and comic and entertainment TV shows, Mexico has arguably been the "cultural imperialist" of Hispanic Latin America. For instance, *Siempre en Domingo*, a weekly musical revue produced by Televisa and hosted by Raúl Velasco from 1969 to 1998, reached an audience of about 420 million television viewers; appearing on this show became a must for musicians and singers from all over Latin America and Spain who were trying to achieve success in the Spanish-language music market.

The Mexican radio industry developed with the government's authorization, growing from four commercial broadcasting stations in

1923 to nineteen in 1929. But when Emilio Azcárraga founded XEW "La Voz de la América Latina desde México" (The Voice of Latin American from Mexico) in 1930, Mexico established the foundation of the broadcasting system that came to dominate Latin American airwaves throughout the 20th century. Azcárraga's affiliation with American networks RCA, NBC, and CBS through the 1940s enabled him to launch a broadcasting empire that controlled almost half the radio stations in Mexico and distributed programming to the Dominican Republic, Honduras, El Salvador, Nicaragua, Costa Rica, Panama, Colombia, Venezuela, Ecuador, Peru, and Uruguay. Complying with early nationalist cultural policies of the Secretaría de Educación Pública (Ministry of Public Education) but also as a strategy to remain independent from his United States associates, Azcárraga designed a unique programming of Mexican music and developed a market that only his broadcasting empire could satisfy (Hayes 2000).

During the 1940s, the Mexican film industry grew strong taking advantage of the vacuum left in Latin America by a U.S. industry focused on local markets and propaganda movies during World War II. Known as the *Época de Oro* (Golden Age) of Mexican cinema, it is characterized by the ubiquitous presence of Mexican music traditions in *comedia rancheras* films; the most privileged genre being *canción ranchera* and its mariachi ensemble. Mariachi became the Mexican symbol it is today largely because of the dynamics between the film and radio industries in those years, an alliance that allowed these industries to support but also to reinvent each other's products.

Media played an essential role in developing icons of national belonging during the consolidation of Mexico's post-revolutionary regime (1930–60), and it has also provided new ones from a transnational perspective today. The *banda* craze of the 1990s owes much to the powerful Mexican American media's ability to influence local broadcasting networks in Mexico and affected the popularization of dance genres like *pasito duranguense* and *quebradita* among Mexicans and Mexican Americans.

The three themes that guide this study of music in Mexico are related. The Mexican media were a powerful force in propagating *indigenismo* and *mestizaje* among the country's population throughout the 20th century. Further, the transnational experience of Mexican emigrants permitted the media to profit from the commercialization of the musical genres and styles they preferred. The daily life experiences of multicultural migrants forces us to rethink the problematic class and ethnic discourses about Mexicans and Mexican culture both in Mexico and the

United States. Finally, cosmopolitanism, understood as the aspirations of individuals to be part of communities that transcend their locality, is a concept that links all three themes together. Cosmopolitanism helps us understand how contemporary genres like *balada*, rock, and *canto nuevo* are reinvented and made meaningful in a variety of contemporary geographic contexts. It also explains the processes of appropriation of genres and styles like *bolero* and *norteña*. Understanding how historical processes of globalization intersect aspirations and desires for cosmopolitan belonging provides a theoretical space in which the three themes overlap. This offers new ways to examine and interpret the power of Mexican musical practices beyond the geographic boundaries of particular ethnic formations or even the Mexican nation-state.

CHAPTER 2

The Transnational Resurgence
of *Son Jarocho*

It is a typical cold and cloudy morning in late November in Chicago. I have difficulty walking on 18th Street as snow and ice have covered the sidewalks, giving the city the distinctive look it will have for the next few months. I turn onto Racine and immediately spot the entrance of Casa Aztlán. I open the door into the lobby where children and their parents are shedding their coats, scarves, and gloves. They then move into the hall and sit in a circle as Raul begins strumming chords on his *requinto jarocho* and Gina sings a children's song that introduces each child by name. Everyone sings and rhythmically claps as Raul and Gina are slowly joined by other members of Jarochicanos, the Chicago-based *son jarocho* youth group. Once the musicians have set the pace of their music they switch to traditional *son jarocho*. The children are invited to step on the *tarima* (wooden dance box) in the middle of the circle and join the performance with their own *zapateado* (heel dancing). The collective performance climaxes with "La bamba," arguably the most famous *son jarocho* song. "Para bailar la bamba se necesita una poca de gracia / una poca de gracia pa' ti y pa' mi / ¡Ay! ¡Arriba y arriba!" (To dance la bamba you need a little bit of grace / a little bit of grace for you and for me / Ay! Higher and higher!). It is wonderful to hear this warm music played with such passion in the middle of the Midwest winter, and even more so to see the youngsters attending the workshop give it a new life so far away from Veracruz where it originated centuries ago.

This workshop, Son Chiquitos (a wordplay that can be translated either as Little Ones *Son* or They Are Little Ones), is led by Raul Fernandez and Gina Gamboa, the founders of Jarochicanos, a group aimed at disseminating *son jarocho* music among Latino youth in

Chicago. Son Chiquitos and Jarochicanos are an indicator of the growing interest in *son jarocho* among Chicago Latino youngsters. In the
last 30 years the genre has given young Mexican Americans in Los
Angeles, Chicago, Seattle, San Antonio, Madison, and New York a way
to identify with and to celebrate the cultural heritage of their parents,
grandparents, and even great-grandparents. Its success here is connected to the rebirth that *son jarocho* has experienced in Mexico since
the late 1970s when Mono Blanco and Siquisirí, and later Chuchumbé,
Los Parientes, Los Cojolites, and Son de Madera, reclaimed *son jarocho*
from the fossilized, postcard version it had become in the "official" stiff,
theatrical performances favored by cultural brokers, media producers,
and ballet *folklórico* proponents. The revitalized movement emphasized
the tradition's social aspects and openness to collective participation.
In this chapter I explore the history of *son jarocho*, show the relationship
between its Mexican renaissance and its increasing presence among
Mexican American communities across the United States, and analyze
the music's performative power in its present diverse social and cultural settings.

THE MEXICAN *SON* COMPLEX

Son jarocho belongs to a larger Mexican musical complex of regional
styles of *sones* such as *son abajeño, son arribeño, son calentano, son de
artesa, son jarocho, son huasteco, son istmeño,* and numerous musical practices of the colonial period (1521–1821) known as *sonecitos
del país* (little *sones* from the countryside). *Sones,* basically meaning
"sounds," "tunes," or songs, are mestizo dance musics developed in
18th-century Mexico mixing Spanish, African, and indigenous music
traditions. They represent the oldest repertory of traditional Mexican
music. Regional *sones* are stylistically distinct but share common elements: they all combine a type of plucked string-based instrumental
ensemble with *zapateado* dance style, an improvisatory singing structure called *copla,* and predominant ternary rhythmic patterns with
frequent *sesquiáltera* or *hemiola* (a rhythmic practice common to many
Spanish and Spanish American musics characterized by a continuous
shift from compound duple to simple triple meters, typically back
and forth from 6/8 to 3/4). Most *son* traditions are participatory in
nature; community members join in dancing and singing at celebrations called *fandangos* which often include musicians from different
bands jamming together.

ACTIVITY 2.1. *As you read about these varieties of son, create a chart for yourself that includes for each these elements: the name(s) of the variety, the region(s) in which it flourishes, the instrumentation for the music, and other information. In this way, you can begin to understand what distinguishes the varieties from each other and also glimpse the richness of the varieties of music in Mexico.*

Sonecitos del país's repertory of popular songs and *jarabes* (multisectioned dances) entered city theaters as part of *entremeses* (one-act comic theatrical performances). Propaganda vehicles of patriotic ideas during the Mexican War of Independence (1810–21), the Mexican-American War (1846–48), and the Franco-Mexican War (1861–67), they remained popular through the end of the 19th century transcending regional boundaries to become Mexico's first nationally popular music. Unlike *sonecitos del país*, other *son* traditions remained localized, acquiring significance as regional cultural manifestations through the 20th century. *Son abajeño*, from the western Mexican states of Colima, Jalisco, Michoacán, and Nayarit, features an ensemble that usually includes two violins, *vihuela*, *guitarra de golpe*, and harp or *guitarrón* (bass guitar) which, with its repertory is the basic source of modern mariachi. The *son arribeño* style from the north central states of Guanajuato, Queretaro, and San Luis Potosí is characterized by two violins, which provide the main melodic and rhythmic elements, *guitarra quinta*, *jarana* and *vihuela*. The Tierra Caliente (Hot Land) region in the western states of Michoacán and Guerrero is home to the *son calentano*. The type of *son calentano* from the Balsas River area features an ensemble of one or two violins, one or several guitars, and a small drum. The one from the Tepalcatepec river region is a larger ensemble called *conjunto de arpa grande* (large harp ensemble) composed of one or two violins, *guitarra de golpe*, *vihuela*, and a large harp that gives the group its name and is also used as a percussion instrument.

Originating in the southern states of Guerrero and Oaxaca's Costa Chica (Small Coast), an area with a strong Afro-Mexican presence, the *son de artesa* is also known as *son de tarima* since it features a wooden platform (*tarima*) where dancers perform rhythmic patterns in *zapateado* style, a percussive component considered an intrinsic stylistic element rather than a simple ornament. Besides the *tarima*, the ensemble includes violin, *cajón* (wooden box), and *charasca* or *guacharasca* (a type of rain stick) or violin, guitar, and drum. The repertoire *artesa* musicians play includes *sones* and *chilenas*. The *son istmeño*, from Oaxaca's Tehuantepec isthmus, is an ensemble of one or several guitars, *requinto*, and occasionally marimba. Due to the area's large Zapotec population, many *sones istmeños* are either in Zapotec language or bilingual. *La huasteca* is a region that intersects the northeastern states of San Luis Potosí, Tamaulipas, Hidalgo, and Veracruz in northeastern Mexico; it gives its name to the *son huasteco* style, played by both its mestizo and indigenous communities, and characterized by an instrumental lineup that includes violin, *jarana*, and *guitarra quinta* or *huapanguera* (after the *huapango*, a common genre in the *son huasteco* repertory). Its most salient features are the virtuoso violin parts and the improvisation among all instruments and singers.

ACTIVITY 2.2. *Do some research about the* chilena *(earlier in the chapter) as a music genre and try to think about it in relation to the story of migratory flows. Where did it come from? Why is it called* chilena? *What other South American dance styles is it related to? What countries claim these dances as "national" symbols?*

STYLE AND PRACTICE IN *SON JAROCHO*

Although sharing many general features with other *son* styles the *son jarocho* features a unique musical structure, improvisatory style, performance practice, and singing tradition. Its origins are in many cities and towns on the Papaloapan River and the Los Tuxtlas area of central and southeastern Veracruz state. This is the state's largest subregion and is called El Sotavento (Where the Winds Blow). Within this cultural complex is the World Heritage town of Tlacotalpan whose historical importance as a commercial port during the 19th century is still celebrated in the *décimas* (a 10-line poetic form) in some older *sones jarochos*. Since 1978, Tlacotalpan has annually hosted a *fandango*, the Encuentro de Jaraneros y Decimistas (Meeting of *Jarana* Players and *Décima* Singers), as part of the celebrations for its patron, the Candelaria Virgin. Figure 2.1 shows the town's main road entrance. Lasting for several days and culminating on February 2 (day of the Candelaria Virgin), it is the most important encounter of *son jarocho* musicians, singers, and dancers, and

FIGURE 2.1.   *Monument to* Son Jarocho *at the entrance of Tlacotalpan, Veracruz.* *(© Ekaterina Pirozhenko. Used by permission of Ekaterina Pirozhenko, 2012.)*

is a pilgrimage destination for professional and aficionado *son jarocho* practitioners from Mexico and the United States. Although this *encuentro*'s original intention was to maintain traditional forms of *son jarocho*, it has become a kaleidoscope of contemporary practices, causing tensions between conservatives wishing to keep *son jarocho* with a fixed repertory and performance practice and those wanting to inject musical elements from other traditions, making it more meaningful to everyday realities and lifestyles.

Despite historical and regional variations, *son jarocho*'s basic ensemble includes *arpa jarocha* (harp), *requinto jarocho*, and *jarana* but rarely the violin, which was included in early 20th-century ensembles. Different local performance traditions may include an assortment of percussion instruments, among them the *quijada de burro* (donkey jaw), *pandero* (tambourine), *tarima*, *cajón*, and *marimbol* or *marímbula* (bass thumb piano). The harp's main role is to provide a strong bass line but it also introduces melodic material based on the song's harmonic progression.

The *requinto jarocho, guitarra de son,* or *guitarra jabalina* is a four-string, guitar-like instrument; its body, neck, and tuning head are carved from a single piece of wood, with the top made out of a thin piece of wood. The slightly raised finger board features guitar-like metallic frets, usually up to the joint of the neck and the body but sometimes also running all the way down to the sound hole. The traditional tuning of both the *requinto jarocho* and the *jarana* was based on a series of intervals between the instruments' open strings. Tuning was not understood as a series of specific pitches, like the contemporary notion of "tuning," and the instruments in the ensemble were tuned to each other as opposed to an external reference. Today, however, many musicians often tune their instruments in relation to specific pitches. The *requinto jarocho* uses nylon strings that could be tuned differently according to the instrument's size, the most common tunings being (from the lower string up) B C F B' or F G C' F', with another possible tuning (E) A D' G' C', with the lower E string optional for the occasional five-string *requinto*. Since the actual pitches may change, the most important aspect of the tuning is the intervallic relation between strings. According to their sizes, the different *requintos* are called *primo* (the smallest one), *punteador*, *medio requinto*, *requinto* (the most common), *cuarta*, *leona*, and *león* (the largest one). The *requinto* is played with a variety of *punteado* (plucking) techniques that involve a type of plectrum called *espiga* (spike) or *pluma* (feather), traditionally made from horn or bone but plastic ones are now quite common. The *requinto's* sound is deep and percussive, usually carrying the melody or providing a continuous melodic accompaniment to the singer; occasionally, it could also be used to strum chords. In southern Veracruz, it is common that an ensemble of *requintos* playing the bass line and melodies would replace the *arpa jarocha*. Figure 2.2 shows Raul Fernandez playing his *requinto*.

The *jarana* is a five-course, guitar-shaped instrument, a course being usually a pair or more of adjacent strings. Like the *requinto jarocho*, it is carved from a single piece of wood (although contemporary instruments may be made from separate pieces, like guitars). The slightly raised fingerboard features 12 metallic frets that very rarely go beyond the body and neck joint. The lowest and highest *órdenes* (courses) are single and the three middle ones are double (a common feature among baroque plucked instruments, the direct ancestors of the *jarana*) which gives the instrument its unique timbral quality. Habitually the unison and octave stringed courses are slightly "out of tune," which creates beating among all the overtones. Practitioners perceive this acoustic phenomenon as the instrument's timbric richness; some of the smaller *jaranas* may have six, five, or four courses. There are three typical tunings; one (A DD GG' BB E), similar to the higher five strings of a standard guitar but with the fourth,

FIGURE 2.2. *Raul Fernandez playing the* requinto jarocho. *(Courtesy of Alejandro L. Madrid)*

third, and second strings as double courses; a second one based on a cycle of fourths (D G′G B′B′ EE C); or a third one based on a C major or a minor chord (G AA E′E CC G). They are all re-entrant tunings (a tuning in which the strings are not ordered from lowest to highest pitch), with an octave stringing in the third.

There are several types of *jaranas*; according to size, they are called *chaquiste*, the smallest one; *mosquito* or *chillador* (squeaker); *primera*; *segunda*; *tres cuartos*; *tercera* (the most common); and *tercerola* (the largest one). The *jarana* produces a very percussive sound and provides the rhythmic and harmonic framework of *son jarocho* as the player produces energetically strummed chords in a variety of rhythmic patterns. These strumming patterns are called *maniqueos* (strokes); the combination of two basic playing techniques—strumming (all strings simultaneously) and *rasgueo* (a roll created by the fingers slowly sweeping across the strings)—and effects such as striking the fingers against the strings or

FIGURE 2.3.   *Anabel Tapia playing the* jarana. *(Courtesy of Alejandro L. Madrid)*

slapping the strings against the fret board offer *jaraneros* (*jarana* play-ers) a large rhythmic and textural palette. The *jarana* sound is so central to the *son jarocho* tradition that the word *jaranero* is actually used as a synonym of *son jarocho* musician. Figure 2.3 shows Anabel Tapia, *jarana* player of the Chicago-based group Tarima Son.

The percussion instruments used in the southern region of Veracruz include *tarima, pandero, quijada de burro,* and *marímbula.* The *tarima* is a wooden platform where couples take turns dancing, joining the musical performance by producing rhythmic patterns via their *zapateado.* This dancing is a social practice fundamental to *son jarocho* as it allows com-munity members to participate, their percussive footwork emphasizing the polyrhythmic character of the music. Figure 2.4 shows *zapateado* on a *tarima.*

The *pandero* is an octagonal hand drum of Spanish origin; the player strikes its leather drumhead or its wooden frame, which includes eight pairs of jingles fixed in slots on each side of the frame. The player com-bines striking the drumhead and the frame with the right hand with

FIGURE 2.4. *The* tarima *of Chicago-based group Tarima Son. (Courtesy of Alejandro L. Madrid)*

shaking the instrument with the left hand to make the jingles rattle. The *quijada de burro,* a percussion instrument of African origin made with the lower jaw of a donkey or horse, is played by hitting the side of the jaw, making the teeth vibrate. An Afro-mestizo large wooden box used in *son de artesa* and other African-influenced musics in Latin America (particularly in Afro-Peruvian music) is the *cajón,* on which the musician usually sits and plays rhythmic patterns on one side of the box. The *marimbol or marímbula* is a thumb piano common in sub-Saharan Africa and the Afro-Caribbean diaspora; in *son jarocho* it plays or reinforces bass lines. The instrument is particularly featured by contemporary Tlacotalpan ensembles. *Marímbulas* often are large wooden boxes with a sound hole on one side and metallic tongues of different sizes attached to a piece of wood above the sound hole. There is no standard *marímbula* in *son jarocho,* for the instrument varies in size and number of tongues, which rarely have a range beyond one octave.

ACTIVITY 2.3. *Investigate what other Afro-Mexican, Afro-Caribbean and Afro-Latin American traditions use the* tarima, *the* cajón, *the* quijada de burro, *and the* marímbula. *Discuss with your teacher and classmates the possible relations between these traditions and* son jarocho.

Harmonically, traditional *sones* are rather simple, often following I-IV-V-I or even I-V-I chord progressions. The complexity of *son jarocho* is in its rhythmic structure and the improvisational character of *requinto* solos and lyrics. With few exceptions (like the famous *sones* "La bamba," "El colás," or "El tilingo lingo") *son jarocho* tends to be in ternary rhythm, in composed duple meter (6/8) with frequent instances of *sesquiáltera* or *hemiola* in the melodic rhythmic structure or the often polyrhythmic instrumental accompaniment. The formal structure of *son jarocho* is strophic and usually alternates calls, responses, and improvisational instrumental sections; "La María Chuchena" offers a good example of this. The sung sections are organized strophically by a principle of call and response in which a soloist (usually the lead *requinto* player) sings a melody (a) that is repeated with different lyrics (a') by the other musicians. After the response, there is a new call based on a slightly different melody (b), and a new response (which in this case is a refrain that is repeated exactly the same at each section's end). The version recorded in the accompanying CD (track 1) is one of the song's many possible versions; most variants keep one or two stanzas and the refrain but add new verses.

ACTIVITY 2.4. *Listen to CD track 1, a recording of "La María Chuchena," and follow its structure (Figure 2.5). The song is divided into three large similarly organized sections. Instrumental solos begin each section, first with the introduction, then an instrumental interlude at 0:48, and another at 1:30. You will notice that all* requinto *solos are improvisations on the same harmonic sequence and their endings elaborations of the same hemiola-based cadence (look at it at the end of measure 16 in Figure 2.6). The companion website has a more detailed analysis of the use of hemiolas in "La María Chuchena." To see how different musicians might expand the song, look on the Internet for other versions, such as the recording by the renowned East Los Angeles-based band Los Lobos.*

During a *fandango* performance, musicians would likely extend the *son* in two ways, one by expanding the instrumental interludes

Time	Music Event	Section	Thematic material	Text	Translation
0	Requinto solo + jarana accompaniment	Introduction			
0:17	Soloist	Call	a	Estaba María Chuchena / sentadita en la barranca / sentadita en la barranca / estaba María Chuchena	María Chuchena was / sitting by the edge of the hill / sitting by the edge of the hill / María Chuchena was
0:25	Choir	Response	a'	Cortando las azucenas / regando las flores blancas / y estaba María Chuchena / sentadita en la barranca	She was cutting lilies / watering the white flowers / María Chuchena was / sitting at the edge of the hill
0:33	Soloist	Call	b	María Chuchena se fue a bañar / a orilla del río, cerca del mar / María Chuchena se estaba bañando / y el pescador la estaba mirando	María Chuchena went to take a bath / by the river, near the sea / María Chuchena was bathing / and a fisherman was looking at her
0:40	Choir	Response	c	Ay, le decía: María, María / no techo la casa, no techo la mía / no techo la casa, no techo la mía / no techo la casa de María García	Ay, he said: María, María / I don't roof the house, I don't roof mine / I don't roof the house, I don't roof mine / I don't roof María García's house

(Continued)

21

(Continued)

Time	Music Event	Section	Thematic material	Text	Translation
0:48	Requinto solo + jarana accompaniment + 2nd requinto solo	Instrumental interlude			
1:02	Soloist	Call	a'	Por aquí pasó volando / una calandria amarilla / y una calandria amarilla / por aquí pasó volando	Flying nearby was / a yellow calandria / a yellow calandria / was flying nearby
1:09	Choir	Response	a'	En el piquito llevaba / una rosa de Castilla / que el viento la deshojaba / como blanca maravilla	In its little beak it had / a Castilla rose / which the wind was defoliating / like a white wonder
1:17	Soloist	Call	b'	María Chuchena bájate al agua/ junto a la proa de mi piragua / María Chuchena bájate al mar / para navegar	María Chuchena come down to the water / by the prow of my boat / María Chuchena come down to the sea / to sail
1:23	Choir	Response	c	Ay, le decía: María, María / no techo la casa, no techo la mía / no techo la casa, no techo la mía / no techo la casa de María García	Ay, he said: María, María / I don't roof the house, I don't roof mine / I don't roof the house, I don't roof mine/ I don't roof María García's house

Time	Instrumentation	Section	Label	Spanish	English
1:30	Requinto solo (without accompaniment)	Instrumental interlude			
1:45	Requinto solo + jarana accomapniment + 2nd requinto solo	Instrumental interlude continues			
1:57	Soloist	Call	a'	Dime que flor te acomoda / para írtela a cortar / para írtela a cortar / dime que flor te acomoda	Tell me which flower you like / to go cut it / to go cut it / tell me which flower you like
2:04	Choir	Response	a'	Azucena y amapola / Amalia, flor de mar / para cuando vengas sola / tengas con quien platicar	Lily and poppy / Amalia, sea flower / so when you come by yourself / you'd have someone to talk to
2:11	Soloist	Call	b	María Chuchena se fue a bañar / a orilla del río, cerca del mar / María Chuchena se estaba bañando / y el pescador la estaba mirando	María Chuchena went to take a bath / by the river, near the sea / María Chuchena was bathing / and a fisherman was looking at her
2:17	Choir	Response	c	Ay, le decía: María, María / no techo la casa, no techo la mía / no techo la casa, no techo la mía / no techo la casa de María García	Ay, he said: María, María / I don't roof the house, I don't roof mine / I don't roof the house, I don't roof mine / I don't roof María García's house

FIGURE 2.5. *Descriptive chart of "La María Chuchena." (Courtesy of Alejandro Madrid)*

FIGURE 2.6. *Instrumental introduction to "La María Chuchena." (Courtesy of Alejandro L. Madrid)*

to allow for more instrumental improvisation as well as *zapateado* by *tarima* performers, another by allowing singers to improvise *coplas* (verses) during the sung sections. On occasion, the call and response style between soloist and choir might be replaced by two singers improvising against each other in a type of *copleros'* (verse improvisers) duel of sorts. These improvisations last from a few minutes to hours depending on the energy developed between *jaraneros, tarimeros,* and *copleros.*

    Coplas follow a traditional poetic form of octosyllabic lines usually organized in quatrains (four lines), although also in sestets (six lines) and occasionally quintains (five lines) and *décimas* (10 lines). Some older *sones* are organized according to *décimas,* a 17th-century Spanish poetic form common to other types of Latin American musics from Cuba, Puerto Rico, the Dominican Republic, Venezuela, Colombia, Chile, Uruguay, and Argentina, but the bulk of the repertory, especially newer songs or older ones with new lyrics, is organized in quatrains.

ACTIVITY 2.5. *The companion website to this book contains more detailed analysis of quatrain strophes in "La María Chuchena." Use that analysis as a model to do some poetic analysis of your own. Find a décima by a contemporary poet such as Guillermo Cházaro Lagos and a 17th-century Spanish décima-based poem by a writer such as Pedro Calderón de la Barca, and compare them.*

Improvising *coplas* is one of the most salient and difficult features of *son jarocho*, separating good from extraordinary performers. The *décima* is no longer the most common poetic form used in *son jarocho*, but because it is the oldest and most traditional, *copleros* are often called *decimistas*. The improvisation of *décimas* is still the ultimate test for a superior *coplero*; so, when they are improvising, seasoned *copleros* humorously mention current events and facts about musicians or people present. These improvised vocal performances are the backbone of a *fandango* event and also the norm when street musicians sing in restaurants or public plazas. Street musicians use numerous formulas by which they might insert customers' names to personalize the *copla*, a practice less appreciated among connoisseurs at a *fandango*, who expect more creative forms of improvisation. Also, among street musicians, rhymes tend to follow simple "abab" patterns, while *fandango* musicians perform more complex *décima* rhyme patterns (e.g., "abbaaccddc" or "abbaaccddcd" or "abbaaccaac"). The *copleros* are central to the *fandango* as their creativity, invention, and wittiness energize other participants (*jaraneros*, *copleros*, and *tarimeros*) and galvanize the crowd, thus shaping the tone and character of the collective performance.

ACTIVITY 2.6. *Search the Internet for videos of fandangos and analyze the dynamics of these collective performances. How do the tarima zapateado rhythms relate to the string instruments? How do tarima dancers and copleros interact?*

SON JAROCHO IN VERACRUZ: A HISTORY OF MIGRATION AND TRANSCULTURATION

Founded in 1519 as Villa Rica de la Vera Cruz (Rich Village of the True Cross), Veracruz is Mexico's first European city, its oldest and largest port, and the point of entry into New Spain, Mexico's name during the Spanish colonial era (1521–1821). Veracruz developed a strong local economy and unique local culture, resulting from the encounter of the locals and the willing—or unwilling—immigrants. Soon, diseases brought by the Spaniards—like smallpox—decimated the native population, leaving the Europeans without labor. This initiated Spain's African slave trade that lasted until 1640, although slavery itself was not officially abolished in Mexico until 1821, after the declaration of independence from Spain. A reduced indigenous population combined with small numbers of Spanish immigrants meant that by end of the 16th century, African slaves outnumbered Spaniards by three to one and Veracruz became home to the largest slave population in New Spain. This slowly reversed after 1640, and processes of transculturation helped develop a unique Mexican culture out of indigenous, Spanish, and African traditions. Veracruz was the first site for cultural encounters fueled by early, influential, and dramatic processes of globalization in the region. These migrations of people and their heritage, and the resulting uneven social dynamics are central in understanding the development of Mexican culture and particularly *jarocho* culture.

I have discussed African influence in *son jarocho* in the use of percussion instruments like the *marímbula* and *quijada de burro*, the polyrhythms and syncopations in the footwork of *tarima* dancers that, tradition says, replaced the drums Africans were forbidden to play. I have noted Spanish influence in terms of instruments, *copla* improvisations, the ubiquitous *hemiola* rhythmic pattern, and remarkably, the survival of the spirit of baroque music in contemporary Mexican popular music traditions. These baroque genres and performance practices are products of the initial encounter of African, Spanish, and indigenous traditions. The *jarana* and *requinto* are not just "guitar-like" instruments; they are direct descendants of the *vihuela* and baroque guitar, brought by the Spaniards to the Americas during the 16th and 17th centuries, for they are built, strung, and played more like those instruments than like the modern guitar. Recent work by Mexican musicologists Antonio Corona Alcalde and Eloy Cruz and the performance project of Tembembe Ensamble Continuo (for whom Cruz plays baroque guitar, "baroque *jarana*," and theorbo) focus on the ways Spanish baroque musical elements were transformed into distinctly Mexican musical traits, and the continuities that *son jarocho* displays between its present and the baroque past.

Fragments of old verses from the *guineos*, *cumbées*, or *zarambeques* (baroque music genres) have been preserved in contemporary *coplas* and quatrains as exemplified by the lyrics of "La María Chuchena" (see the companion website). These poetic fragments in contemporary *sones jarochos* join other 17th-century survivors such as harmonic sequences that identify different musical forms in many cases nearly unaltered in the chordal progressions played by *jaraneros*. Furthermore, Corona Alcalde suggests that the ways in which *jaranas* and *requintos* are played resemble baroque performance practices; *requintos* continuously improvising variations over a song's harmonic progression (as heard in "La María Chuchena") is reminiscent of the way that 16th-century *vihuelistas* developed *diferencias* (sets of variations on a given theme or harmonic sequence) (1995: 50). Corona Alcalde also describes the basic strumming technique used by *jarana* players today as an outgrowth of techniques shown in surviving 17th- and 18th-century manuscripts in Mexico, such as the Saldívar Codex IV (music by the Spanish baroque guitarist Santiago de Murcia). Corona Alcalde explains that these basic patterns are ornamented in complex ways by contemporary *jarana* players following standard baroque practices to embellish guitar strumming (called *repicci* or *repiques*) described in Giovanni Paolo Foscarini's guitar treatise *Il primo, secondo, e terzo libro della chitarra spagnola* (ca. 1629) (1995: 51–57). Evidence of the practice of *repique* is also found in the lyrics of "El tilingo lingo," a traditional *son jarocho*; its refrain—"Ay repica, pica, pica / repica y repiqueteando / que bonitas, que bonitas / todas las que están bailando" (Ay, re-strum, strum, strum / re-strum and re-strumming / how beautiful, how beautiful / all of those girls dancing)—invites *jarana* players to vigorously strum their instruments at the sight of the ladies dancing on the *tarima*.

Eloy Cruz and Tembembe Ensamble Continuo members (see Figure 2.7) base their project on some issues raised by Corona Alcalde, although they argue that the most compelling evidence of continuities between baroque and *son jarocho* practices is in the repertory itself. Cruz states that some *sones jarochos* still maintain the same titles, lyrics (or fragments), and music from surviving 18th-century sources (manuscripts, and printed editions of scores and tablatures). The ensemble's CD *Laberinto de la guitarra* (2004) combines baroque music performed directly from tablatures with *sones jarochos* performed with traditional *jarocho* instruments. After finding a *son* that corresponds to a specific baroque dance, they adapt it into a single composition so they can move seamlessly from one to the other within a single performance. A good example is the ensemble's recording of de Murcia's "La Jota" combined with the traditional *son* "La María Chuchena" a detailed analysis of which is in the companion website.

FIGURE 2.7.   *Tembembe Ensamble Continuo. (Used by courtesy of Tembembe)*

ACTIVITY 2.7.   *Listen to CD track 2, a recording of "La Jota" / "María Chuchena," and follow the listening chart of the song in the website. Discuss in class how the song exemplifies the practices discussed in the textbook.*

THE RISE OF *SON JAROCHO* AS A MEXICAN NATIONAL ICON

El Gran Café de la Parroquia is one of the most traditional restaurants and cafes in Veracruz city. Founded in 1858 and established under its current name in 1938, it has been the meeting place for middle-class locals, initially mostly men, to discuss everything from regional and national politics to the latest international financial crash (usually imagining Veracruz at the center of these affairs). These fantastic conversations often start with seafood soup, *picadas, gordas,* and Zaraza Vargas (a local soda), and conclude over *bombas* and *café lechero,* the sweet coffee with milk for which *la parroquia* (as locals call it) is famous. The final

FIGURE 2.8.   Jaraneros *at the Gran Café de la Parroquia, Veracruz City, Mexico.*
(© Ekaterina Pirozhenko. Used by courtesy of Ekaterina Pirozhenko, 2012.)

ingredient is live *son jarocho* music played by musicians wearing the stereotypical *jarocho* outfit: men in a white *guayabera* –also called *filipina* (Philippine)– white pants, *jarocho* hat, and a red bandanna around their neck; women wearing a long-skirted white dress and apron. These are the outfits that 20th-century ballet *folklórico* performances made famous as symbols of Veracruz. Figure 2.8 shows *son jarocho* musicians at El Gran Café de la Parroquia.

The restaurant musicians' repertory includes customer pleasers, the tradition's greatest hits ("La bamba," "El colás," "El tilingo lingo," "El cascabel") even though this type of *son jarocho* has become a postcard for the tradition at large, something that most traditional practitioners are alienated from and often make fun of. When talking about what audiences expect from a *son jarocho* group, a Mexican *tarima* dancer living in New York once told me, "what happens with traditional *son jarocho* in Mexico is that not a lot of people know it, although it is slowly becoming more and more popular; for example, when Mexicans invite us to perform at their parties they expect the *jarochos* dressed in white, right? They expect what we in the *jaranero* movement call the *marisqueros* (Spanish *marisco*, or seafood), the *son jarocho* that's played at seafood restaurants." Why and how did this commercialized *son jarocho* become a symbol of local identity?

As mentioned in Chapter 1, numerous private and government-sponsored projects attempted to define icons of Mexican identity at the revolution's end (1921). In the 1930s and 1940s it was mariachi music that symbolized a cohesive Mexican identity, with the *jarabe tapatío* as the quintessential Mexican folk dance. With the growing power of film and radio, this musical representation of the nation dominated ideas about Mexico within and beyond its borders. Private and public institutions channeled this to strengthen the tourist industry as a cornerstone of Mexican development. However, in the late 1940s, *son jarocho* became an ubiquitous presence in these representations of Mexicanness. A major promoter to develop a tourist industry was Miguel Alemán Valdés, who was elected president of Mexico in 1946. The first civilian president since the Mexican revolution, Alemán pushed for economic and political modernization that included attracting foreign investment and protecting Mexican industries; tourism was central to this project. Theoretically, Alemán's administration favored a representation of Mexico as a country whose modernity was supported by tradition, but in practice the focus remained on "old" Mexico. The contradiction is understood since the goal of tourist industries is to offer a unique product, so creating an image of Mexico as a tourist culture by promoting the country's many and "exotic" traditions offered the desired effect of uniqueness. Although costumes, folk dances, and colonial and precolonial architecture from all over Mexico were included in these representations, cultural objects and manifestations from the state of Veracruz were privileged.

ACTIVITY 2.8. *Investigate how the Alemán administration made an ideological shift from previous Mexican administrations and how this changed the political and economic development of the country. Prepare to discuss this in class.*

The sudden rise of Veracruz to a central place in the discourse on Mexican national identity is easily explainable in political terms, for presidents Miguel Alemán Valdés (1946–52) and Adolfo Ruiz Cortines (1952–58), both of whom established and managed the new national economic agenda, were from Veracruz. In Mexico's 1950s political system of uncontested presidential authority and limitless power, all things *jarocho* became fashionable and *son jarocho*, one of Alemán's favorite musics, became pervasive in Mexican politics after his 1946 political campaign. During his administration, the famous *son* "La bamba" became popular in Veracruz and beyond; it was labeled *Himno Alemanista* (Alemán's anthem) first, and *Himno Jarocho* (Jarocho anthem) soon after. Older practitioners interviewed by Randall Kohl state that *son jarocho* was practically dead in Veracruz until politicians in the 1940s, especially Alemán, started requesting this music (Kohl 2007: 51–59).

The attention to *son jarocho* and Mexican folk musics and cultures resulting from the national tourism project was also detrimental, fossilizing them into "official" banners of national identity. One of Alemán's first presidential acts was the creation of Mexico's Instituto Nacional de Bellas Artes (National Fine Arts Institute); one of its goals is to oversee the preservation, protection, and promotion of the country's artistic heritage. An arm of the government's nationalist politics, the institute's music center and dance academy became allies in constructing Mexican icons that would support the larger tourist project. The creation in 1952 and subsequent international success of Amalia Hernández's Ballet Moderno de México (later called Ballet Folklórico de México) engaged the type of folk imagery needed both by tourist policies and the nascent TV industry, and was key in taking folk music practices out of their cultural context and making them tourist-type stage attractions. Ballet *folklórico* companies also became popular among middle-class Mexicans who often sent their children to folk dance lessons.

ACTIVITY 2.9. *Search the Internet for videos of ballet* folklórico *performances by Amalia Hernández's company. Prepare to discuss in class how different these performances are from traditional* fandangos.

Among Mexican Americans, ballet *folklórico* companies became sites for the performance of heritage and loyalty to their parents' and grandparents' country. These institutions created the stereotypes that contemporary traditional *son jarocho* practitioners endearingly but belittlingly call *los marisqueros*; stereotypes whose national and international success accompanied neglect for actual countryside *fandango* practices that did not follow this typecasting and thus were considered lacking sophistication and refusing modernization. Nevertheless, the symbolic power and cultural capital of ballet *folklórico* practices have played a decisive role in the contemporary renaissance of *son jarocho* among Mexicans and Mexican Americans.

THE TRANSNATIONAL RESURGENCE OF *SON JAROCHO*

The Mexican economic crisis of the mid- to late 1970s was harsh on peasants and rural communities. Veracruz state suffered dramatically, leading to massive migration, especially from the Sotavento region into urban areas. Many musicians who migrated to Veracruz and other cities worked as street musicians, although a few were able to get part-time teaching positions in music or dance at Casas de Cultura (Cultural Centers) and other government-sponsored community workshops. In 1977, a group of musicians founded Mono Blanco, a band intended to preserve traditional *son jarocho* as a communitarian practice. Mono Blanco combined the experience of seasoned, older musicians, and their younger apprentices who were also savvy cultural promoters. These younger musicians gained the sponsorship of important cultural institutions of Veracruz state, which allowed them to make performance tours in the state and beyond, and let them organize local music and dance workshops and *fandangos*.

The Mono Blanco activities coincided with a movement in Mexico City to reaffirm traditional Latin American music (see Chapter 7), a result of the populist politics of President Luis Echeverría in the early 1970s; the increasing presence and cultural influence of exiles from dictatorships in Chile, Argentina, and Uruguay; and the fervor for Latin American unity stoked by the Cuban revolution. To position Mexico within this cosmopolitan Latin Americanist movement, urban Mexican musicians and cultural brokers turned to the country's traditional musics beyond the official ballet-*folklórico* representations. Their initiatives were also sponsored both privately and by government institutions in the late 1970s and early 1980s. Meetings of traditional musicians were organized around the country; new groups (like El Chuchumbé, Los Parientes, or Son de Madera) appeared, making Mono Blanco's mission their own. One of the events founded at the time, Tlacotalpan's Encuentro de Jaraneros y Decimistas, has survived and thrived to this day, becoming, as previously noted, a kind of *son jarocho* mecca.

In the late 1980s and 1990s, interest in *son jarocho* shifted from preservation toward experimentation. Musicians rediscovered Afro-mestizo instruments such as the *marímbula* and incorporated new elements such as the blues scale in *requinto* improvisations and instruments like the *quijada de burro*, the congas, and the *cajón* from African American, Afro-Caribbean, and Afro-Peruvian musics. These practices reestablished and reinforced the connection of *son jarocho* to the larger historical complex of African diasporic culture and, after decades of an official racial discourse (*mestizaje*) that effectively rendered blackness invisible among Mexicans, reinstated Mexico as an essential historical pathway to the dissemination and transculturation of African culture in the Americas.

In 1987, the box office hit film *La Bamba*, by Mexican American director Luis Valdéz, told the story of 17-year-old Mexican American rock 'n' roll star Ritchie Valens. A defining scene shows Ritchie and his brother traveling south of the Mexican border to a brothel in Tijuana. While his brother is interested in Ritchie getting intimate with the local ladies, Ritchie appears more absorbed with the brothel's band playing "La bamba." Fascinated by the song, he stands by the stage and starts following the musicians' harmonic sequences on his own guitar. When Richie returns to Los Angeles, he and his producer decide to include a rock 'n' roll version of "La bamba" as the B-side of his second single, "Donna." Valdez's film suggests that Valens's decision to record "La bamba" resulted from a sense of regained Mexican pride after his trip to Tijuana, but in real life Valens already knew the song as it was frequently played by his relatives at family gatherings in Los Angeles. Nevertheless, the film helps us better understand two important moments in Mexican Americans' historical relationship with *son jarocho*. One, the release of Valens's "La bamba" in 1958, which introduced the song to a large audience in the United States, coincided with the popularization of the song in Mexico as an almost "unofficial" Mexican anthem. Second, when the film was released in 1987 it helped solidify the *son jarocho* movement among Mexican Americans in Los Angeles, and ignite interest in it among other Mexican American communities in the United States.

ACTIVITY 2.10.   *Search the Internet for videos of traditional or ballet* folklórico *renditions of "La bamba" and compare them to Ritchie Valens's rock 'n' roll version. What did Valens change and what did he retain in his version?*

Ritchie Valens introduced "La bamba" to United States audiences in the late 1950s by "dressing it up" as rock 'n' roll, the music style that was becoming popular; this illustrates how Mexican Americans struggled to conform to mainstream United States culture so as to be considered Americans. Only in the 1970s, at the height of the Chicana/o civil rights movement, with its re-signification and celebration of Mexican expressive culture as a marker of identity, did *son jarocho* gain followers among Mexican Americans as a symbol of resistance against an American mainstream that refused to accept them as equals. *Son jarocho* entered the Mexican American imagination through ballet *folklórico* lessons, which became increasingly prominent among Mexican Americans during the 1970s and 1980s, developing into spaces for the performance and celebration of a unique Mexican American identity. Ballet *folklórico*'s fossilized nationalist rhetoric in Mexico was transformed by Mexican Americans to fit their own political agendas.

An early example of this politically nuanced appropriation of *son jarocho* is the work of the East Los Angeles-based band Los Lobos, who play the Mexican musicians at the Tijuana brothel in Valdez's film *La Bamba*. The movie's title, originally *Come On, Let's Go*, after Valens's first single, was changed because the presence of Los Lobos in the movie indicated that a focus on "La bamba" would resonate with the interest on *son jarocho* among Mexican Americans at the time. The success of the movie and the Los Lobos soundtrack recording of "La bamba," number one in the pop music charts for three weeks, galvanized this interest and provided for further commercial success of *son jarocho*-related endeavors such as Los Lobos' Grammy-Award winning album, *La Pistola y El Corazón* (1989), which features two *sones jarochos* among other types of traditional Mexican music. Steve Loza suggests that this recording and their subsequent national concert tour exposed audiences to Los Lobos' modernized and eclectic version of *son jarocho*, by replacing traditional instruments according to the band's needs (1992: 192) and even including English lyrics at times, such as in their guest performance on *Sesame Street*.

Many Mexican Americans who grew up on rock and other U.S. popular music became interested in *son jarocho* precisely because bands like Los Lobos presented it as a modernized musical form that spoke to their own lives in the United States. Raul Fernandez, from Chicago's *son jarocho* band Son del Viento, recalls that he became interested in *son jarocho* after listening to Zazhil (a Mexican band led by Víctor Pichardo) play modernized versions of Mexican *sones* with electric instruments, congas, keyboards, saxophones, and drum set (they branded their style "progressive *son*"). In the early 1980s Zazhil played for Amparo Ochoa, one of the leading figures of the Latin American music movement in Mexico, and first performed in Chicago in 1990, a few years after the Old Town School of Music first invited Mono Blanco to concertize and to teach *son jarocho* workshops in the city. The modern sound of Zazhil and the initial work by Mono Blanco established the foundations of a vigorous *son jarocho* movement in Chicago.

Musicians like Raul Fernandez, first attracted to *son jarocho* by the modern sound of Los Lobos and Zazhil, soon began exploring its traditional aspects. In 1993 Víctor Pichardo and Juan Dies started the Chicago-based band Sones de México, that plays all types of Mexican *sones* but was primarily interested in recovering the collective and communitarian aspect of the *fandango* experience. The emphasis on the *fandango* by Sones de México and other late 1990s and early 2000s *son jarocho* bands such as Tarima Son, Son del Viento, or A Flor de Piel; the influence of Mexican bands such as Mono Blanco, Los Cojolites, Chuchumbé, and Son de Madera performing in Chicago; and the work in K-12 schools and community centers by many band musicians generated interest among Chicago's Mexican American youth in *son jarocho* as something relevant to their lives.

This awakening also took place in cities like Los Angeles, Madison, San Antonio, and Seattle where local bands have emerged—Quetzal from Los Angeles is possibly the most prominent one—and local musicians have developed links with Mexican traditional groups, even traveling to Tlacotalpan to participate in the Encuentro Nacional de Jaraneros y Decimistas. But there is a difference in the Mexican American *son jarocho* movement: while its players acknowledge that the tradition comes from Veracruz, they understand that it is re-signified in the United States according to the realities of the different Mexican American communities, and often the ethnic Latinos, who play it. This is a process of transculturation by which *son jarocho* has become something uniquely representative of the Mexican American and even Latino experience. Such is the case of the many youth groups that take this music and make it their own, one of which is Chicago's Jarochicanos.

According to Gina Gamboa, projects like Jarochicanos and Son Chiquitos have been embraced by the Mexican American and Latino communities because they preserve and celebrate Mexican culture—not only music but also the Spanish language—and provide a space for the continuous development of unique multicultural and political alliances among different Mexican American and Latino groups. Maya Fernandez, *jarana* player, singer, and *tarimera* for Son del Viento, points out that Jarochicanos is strongly influenced by the political needs and everyday lives of their young Latino members. The musical experimentation among Jarochicano members who introduce elements from African American hip-hop and Puerto Rican *bomba* to traditional *son jarocho* should be seen as a response to their multicultural reality as American youth and their recognition that many of the problems faced by Mexican Americans in Chicago are shared by the Puerto Rican and African American communities. The intersection of these ethnic groups occurs in neighborhoods like Little Village, Pilsen, or Humboldt Park and on the stages often shared by the young musicians from these communities. That Mexican American and Latino communities across the United States return to the same traditional forms of *son jarocho* has allowed a common repertory and performance style among musicians in California, Illinois, Texas, Florida, and Wisconsin. Son Solidario (Solidarian Son) is the name taken by young *son jarocho* musicians from these states when they gather at politically progressive events such as the United States Social Forum, at protests against the School of the Americas, or in support of the Farm workers Freedom March. Sharing a common *son jarocho* background has allowed them all to perform together in support of common causes, singing *coplas* (improvised or prepared in advance) that reflect upon the political causes at stake.

ACTIVITY 2.11.   *Search the Internet for videos of Son Solidario at the events mentioned earlier. Analyze the particularities of these* fandangos. *How do they differ from* fandangos *in Mexico? How do their lyrics reflect the political causes they support?*

The hybrid musical forms being forged at these points of cultural and political intersection bear witness to the transnational and transcultural crossings that have characterized the Latin American experience in general and Mexican culture in particular throughout their histories. They also challenge the shortcomings of Mexican *mestizaje* discourses by reestablishing the cultural connection between *son jarocho* and the African diaspora in both historical and contemporary contexts. As such, contemporary *son jarocho* and the experience of contemporary Mexican people are understood in the transnational dialogues this music helps to establish between local Mexican communities, national Mexican discourses, and Mexican American life beyond the boundaries of the Mexican nation-state.

CHAPTER 3

Bolero: Cosmopolitanism and the Mexican Romantic Song until the 1960s

It is June 26, 1992, and Mexico City's majestic Auditorio Nacional is filled to capacity. More than 9,000 people impatiently await the beginning of Luis Miguel's concert. The lights in the auditorium slowly fade as the band starts playing a rhythmic instrumental introduction. The musicians wear matching white silk shirts and black pants and are distributed over a two-flight stage set divided by a staircase: guitar and bass on the ample lower level, the rest of the instruments on the second level—two trumpets and a saxophone to the right, a synthesizer and a drummer to the left—and behind them two female backup singers wearing revealing but still stylish black tight shorts and blouses, one on each side of the stage. The saxophone plays a repeated lick punctuated by the trumpets, harmonized by the synthesizer, and rhythmically embellished by the funky rhythmic drive of drummer, guitarist, and bass player. After a few minutes, a white spotlight illuminates center stage; Luis Miguel appears at the top of the staircase and for a few seconds the uproar from the audience drowns out the music. Luis Miguel, wearing an elegant suit, descends the stairs, walks across the stage, and bows to his frantic fans. He is handsome, elegant, and charismatic; his legendary smile further mesmerizes the audience. A staff member gives him a microphone and he starts singing "Oro de ley" (Solid Gold), one of his most popular Latin pop hits. The first part of the concert consists of this type of Latin pop songs that have made Luis Miguel one of the most popular singers in Latin America. The second half slowly changes the hyperkinetic atmosphere of his Latin pop for a more introspective and intimate mood as he sings modern arrangements of well-known traditional *boleros* from his album

Romance (1991). The band is joined by a larger string ensemble. The long vocal lines and soaring melodies typical of the *bolero* genre provide a perfect vehicle to demonstrate his vocal abilities and the range of his emotional expression. From the powerful and emotional vibrato in the climax of Álvaro Carrillo's "La mentira" (The Lie) to the intimate whispering at the end of Armando Manzanero's "No sé tú" (I Don't Know About You), the audience is exposed to a side of Luis Miguel's artistic personality not exploited so prominently in his early career. Their enthusiastic response indicates that the fans also love this new facet. You can see Luis Miguel in concert in Figure 3.1.

El Sol (The Sun), as he is billed by his marketing team, or "Luismi," as he is known by his adoring fans throughout Latin America, has been one of the most popular and successful Latin American singers of the last 30 years. Born in San Juan, Puerto Rico, in 1970 and raised in Mexico, Luis Miguel started singing professionally as a child. He released his first album at age 11, and by 15 he was a Grammy recipient and an award-winning singer at Italy's San Remo Festival and

FIGURE 3.1.   *Luis Miguel sings. (© Neal Preston/CORBIS)*

Chile's Viña del Mar Festival. By the time of the Auditorio Nacional concert of June 26, 1992, Luis Miguel was well on his way to becoming the huge international star he is today. Yet this concert was particularly significant as it marked an important shift in his career; he went from singing mostly Latin pop to largely focusing on modern arrangements of traditional *bolero*, a genre that had reached the peak of its popularity in the middle of the 20th century. Luis Miguel's career was supported from the beginning by Televisa, the powerful Mexican media conglomerate, crucial to his early internationalization. In fact, the repertory he favors is a good example of the transnational music that media have helped to represent as cosmopolitan since the late 1920s.

The music performed at the June 26, 1992, concert featured Luis Miguel's core repertoire, based on Latin pop, *balada*, and *bolero*. These three related genres belong to a common romantic song complex and are traceable to early 20th-century Mexico and the Caribbean, although other international influences, especially from the United States, have also been central in shaping them. Besides the romantic character of the lyrics, *bolero*, *balada*, and Latin pop also share a cosmopolitan elegance and refinement.

A few years ago, an American friend who heard Luis Miguel at a concert in the United States told me his greatest surprise was that the singer looked like a "business man," referring to his habit of always wearing expensive designer suits on stage. For someone familiar with the long musical tradition to which Luis Miguel belongs and the sense of class and sophistication often attached to it, from Agustín Lara to Armando Manzanero to José José and Emmanuel, his choice of stage clothes is not surprising; it is part of the cosmopolitan appeal of the romantic song tradition.

The association of the *bolero* with things cosmopolitan and urban was created and recreated beginning with the early development of the Mexican radio, recording, and film industries in the 1920s and 1930s; this was in opposition to the type of countryside "authenticity" associated with the different *son* traditions and their offspring, mariachi and *ranchera* music. In fact, the romantic song has more in common with the traditional pop and vocal music of Frank Sinatra and Dean Martin than it does with the traditional Mexican *son* discussed in Chapter 2. Nevertheless, it is sturdily Mexican as much as a transnational experience, evident through its long history of flowing exchanges between Mexico, the United States, the Caribbean, and the rest of Ibero-America.

ACTIVITY 3.1. *Search the Internet for a video of Luis Miguel's live performance of "Será que no me amas," and compare it to The Jacksons' "Blame It on the Boogie." How is Luis Miguel's performance paying homage to Michael Jackson? What elements in Luis Miguel's body movement are borrowed from Michael Jackson's performance style or musical personae? How is the musical arrangement inspired by The Jacksons' funk style? Is Luis Miguel's performance an imitation or is it an appropriation that gives new meaning to these moves and sounds in a new cultural context? Are covers just imitations or are they also creative projects? Prepare to discuss in class.*

THE BASIC STYLISTIC FEATURES
OF A TRANSNATIONAL GENRE

Many are familiar with the name *bolero* through Maurice Ravel's famous orchestral composition inspired by an older traditional Spanish dance in triple meter, not to be confused with the Latin American genre, characterized by duple meter. Other than their name and Spanish origin, these genres do not share common stylistic features. The Latin American *bolero* is a type of urban romantic song popular throughout the Spanish-speaking world for over a century. Although Puerto Ricans claim it as theirs, it more likely originated toward the end of the 19th century in eastern Cuba and quickly spread throughout the Caribbean and Mexico.

Despite the *bolero*'s many stylistic transformations in its long history of crossing boundaries, some early basic musical and thematic characteristics define it as a *mestizo* genre. One of its basic features—especially of early *boleros*—is the so-called *cinquillo cubano* (Cuban quintuplet), a syncopated group of five notes seen in Figure 3.2. This pattern is usually played by a gourd scraper and is used as a timeline or underlying repeated rhythmic pattern that provides the rhythmic foundation of the genre. Besides the use of the *cinquillo*, early *boleros* also feature the *clave*, the timeline seen in Figure 3.3 that is common to a lot of Caribbean-influenced music.

The use of timelines derives from musical practices common to many West African traditions. These timelines, combined with a European instrumental ensemble (sometimes guitars, sometimes piano-based ensembles, as well as larger orchestral formats) and a rich harmonic

FIGURE 3.2.   *Cuban* cinquillo *pattern used in early* boleros.

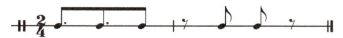

FIGURE 3.3.   *Clave rhythmic pattern used in early* boleros.

style borrowed from the European art music tradition, then from jazz and U.S. big bands, make the *bolero* into a perfect example of the cultural syncretism that characterizes Latin American culture in general, and Caribbean culture in particular. Usually, the *bolero* has two basic sections (A and B) that could be organized in a multiplicity of ways (ABAB, AABB, ABA, etc.), and a large variety of internal organizing principles within each section. Some of these features may be noticed in Guty Cárdenas' "Pasión" (CD track 3).

> **ACTIVITY 3.2.** *Following the charts and analysis provided in the companion website, listen to Guty Cárdenas' "Pasión." Discuss in class the main musical elements of the song.*

Thematically, the genre focuses on romantic tribulations such as forbidden love, betrayal, deception, or the sadness for a lost lover. However, there are also some patriotic or political-critique songs (Eduardo Saborit's "Cuba que linda es Cuba" or Rafael Hernández's "Lamento borincano"). Generally, the lyrics of *boleros* are gender neutral although it is often the male perspective that prevails. The overall character of *boleros* tends to be dramatic in both lyrics and music; one could possibly argue that *boleros* are in a way self-contained dramas.

The cosmopolitan character of the *bolero* is apparent not only in the composers' and arrangers' interest on sophisticated harmonies or possibly the echoes of Italian dramatic theater, but also in the popularization of the genre with its concern with refined language and lyrics. The elegance and cosmopolitanism of Latin American *Modernista* poetry (poets like Rubén Darío or Manuel Gutiérrez Nájera) was a source of inspiration for *bolero* composers in Cuba as well as the rest of Latin America. Most Cubans acknowledge that even if the *bolero* was born in Cuba, it was in Mexico where it became what it is today. This is not to say that the Mexican *bolero* is more "authentic" than any other; what it means is that due to the powerful and influential Mexican radio, film, and recording industries it was the Mexican version of the *bolero* that became more popular throughout the Americas from the 1930s to the 1960s.

THE *BOLERO* IN MEXICO: THE TROVA YUCATECA TRADITION

Historically, the cultural and economic ties between Cuba (especially Havana) and Mexico (particularly Veracruz and the Yucatan peninsula) have been very strong. During the colonial period, Veracruz was the ordinary port of departure for those returning to Spain, while the Gulf Stream made a visit to Havana an obligatory part of the trip. Soon, commercial routes were established and the continuous flow of goods and people between Mexico and Cuba became central to shaping both cultures. Economic, political, and cultural relations between Yucatán (especially Mérida, the state's capital) and Cuba were close and continuous during the colonial period and intensified toward the late 19th century when many members of Cuba's elite fled during its wars of independence and established a large and influential community in Mérida. This allowed for continuous exchanges between the two countries, with a steady flow of merchandise, people, ideas, and cultural goods, among them, music.

ACTIVITY 3.3. *Locate Mérida and the port of Progreso in Yucatán in Figure 1.1. Notice the distance between the Yucatán peninsula and Mexico City, how isolated this region is from central Mexico, and how Yucatán's closeness to Cuba and the Caribbean makes it part of the same cultural area.*

The *bolero* arrived in Mexico at the turn of the 19th century via theater troupes, musicians, and sheet music as part of a transnational process of modernization triggered by the Industrial Revolution and termed "19-century globalization." The *bolero*, together with the Cuban *habanera*, the Colombian *bambuco* and *pasillo*, and the Argentinean tango became the central genres in the musical repertoire of several generations of Yucatecan songwriters known collectively as Trova Yucateca (Yucatecan Song). In all cases, the imported genres were transformed into new ones. The habanera became the *danza* (dance) and later the *canción mexicana* (Mexican song); the *bambuco* and *pasillo*, with their polyrhythmic character—simple triple (3/4) and compound duple (6/8) meters at the same time—influenced the *clave yucateca*. Although the *bolero*'s name remained the same in Mexico, it underwent stylistic transformations as it was adapted to Mexican tastes in different places and at different moments. The generation of musicians and poets who established the Trova Yucateca was largely active from the late 19th century until the early 1920s. It was with the second generation of Trova Yucateca singers that the *bolero* was adopted as a central part of their repertory. This coincided with the end of the armed phase of the Mexican revolution in 1920, which drastically transformed the face of the country, a circumstance crucial for the reception of the *bolero* and its early success in the 1920s and 1930s.

By the 1920s, the long revolutionary war had shattered Mexico's economy. This affected people across class divides but was particularly harsh for peasants and farmers in the countryside who were forced to abandon their rural lifestyles and migrate to the cities to find jobs. The number of inhabitants in urban areas grew exponentially during the first decades of the 20th century; for example, the population of Mexico City quadrupled while that of Mérida almost tripled between 1900 and 1930. The *bolero*, the newcomer among music genres in Mexico, became the soundtrack for these migrants' new agitated urban life.

Ricardo Palmerín, who moved to Mérida from a smaller Mayan village in the early 1920s, was one of the most famous songwriters from the Golden Age of Trova Yucateca. As the most prominent songwriter in Mérida, Palmerín was very influential on younger musicians, composers, and singers, one of whom was Augusto Alejandro "Guty" Cárdenas. Although Cárdenas had a short life, he became a prominent songwriter among the Yucatecan *troveros* and one of the most influential figures in the nascent entertainment industry in Mexico City at the end of the 1920s. The combination of his outstanding talent, good looks, and international support from the emerging recording and radio industries made him into the first Mexican entertainment superstar. Figure 3.4 shows Guty Cárdenas at the height of his career.

Guty Cárdenas grew up in a family for whom playing music was the natural way to spend their leisure time. Regardless of his musical talent, the profession of musician was not seen favorably in an

FIGURE 3.4.   *Guty Cárdenas. (Centro de Investigación Musical "Gerónimo Baqueiro Foster.")*

upper-middle-class family, and Guty was sent to Mexico City to study accounting with the expectation that he would return to Mérida to manage the family business. He returned, but only to inform his family of his decision to become a professional songwriter. In 1927, Guty moved to Mexico City and made his first recordings for the local label Huici; his quick career to stardom started. In 1928, Guty was hired to sing at Hispanic radio stations in New York City where he recorded the bulk of his discography on the Brunswick and Columbia labels. He also played small singing roles in U.S. movies targeting Spanish-speaking audiences. In 1932, Guty returned to Mexico continuing his musical activities until he was murdered in a bar in 1933 at the peak of his popularity.

One of the secrets of Guty's success was his ability to assimilate influences and give new meaning to the many genres popular in Yucatán and Mexico City in the 1920s. This is particularly evident in his use of the *bolero*. Guty's renderings of *boleros* (including his own *bolero* compositions) were very influential in how the genre was appropriated by Mexico City musicians. Although Guty only composed seven such compositions, they feature elements that link the early Cuban style to Mexican *boleros* from the 1930s and 1940s, showing many elements common to the Cuban tradition, especially the *cinquillo* and clave patterns, which slowly disappeared in later Mexican reincarnations of the genre.

ACTIVITY 3.4. *Search the Internet for one bolero from the Trova Cubana tradition (Pepe Sánchez, Sindo Garay, Rosendo Ruiz, Alberto Villalón, or Manuel Corona) and compare it to the early Mexican boleros by Guty Cárdenas and Agustín Lara (next section). Analyze their musical similarities and differences, paying particular attention to rhythmic, melodic, and harmonic features, instrumentation, and form.*

Guty Cárdenas' "Pasión" (Passion) exemplifies the type of Yucatecan *bolero* embraced by Mexico City audiences in the late 1920s (CD track 3). You can find a detailed musical analysis of "Pasión" in the companion website. "Pasion's" lyrics, written by Mérida-based poet Luis Rosado Vega, are full of Orientalist imagery such as "Zegrí eyes" (Zegrí is a royal line from the Granada Sultanate), "fire from Orient," "pearls from Hormuz" (a port between the Persian Gulf and the Gulf of Oman), and "silk from Ophir" (a biblical port famous for its commerce). This imagery is reminiscent of the Orientalist obsession of *Modernista* poets and illustrates the thematic connections between early *bolero* lyrics and this literary movement.

Although the gender of the lover who inspired the song is never actually disclosed, we may assume that it is a female, based on the production context (male lyricist, male composer, and male performer), the male-centered social order of the time, and the imagery used to describe the lover's body. Furthermore, when studying the lyrics in relation to gender one sees the connection between the process of presenting oriental cultures as the Other and the process of objectifying female subjects and seeing them also as the Other within Western culture, dichotomies that the *bolero* clearly reinforced in the Mexican context. This Orientalist imagery always describes a fragment of the female anatomy; the "pearls from Hormuz" refer to her teeth, the "silk from Ophir" to the soft skin of her forehead, and her black eyes are described as "Zegrí," bearing "Oriental fire." This marginalizes the woman, not only reducing her to fragments of her body, neglecting her subjectivity, and reinforcing her as an object in everyday discourse (this is not unique to *bolero* lyrics but is a common feature of Western poetry), but also homologizes the female body with an unknown and exotic land. Every such process implies the imposition of negative connotations onto the Other, but also constructs that Other into an object of desire. In the case of "Pasión," the desire for an exotic, Oriental Other is a metaphor of the lust for the female body expressed in phrases like "Which ardent drop did I sip when kissing you?" "to follow you, to adore you, I have given up everything, my whole being," or "let me kiss your black eyes until I die." This song is a good example of how desire, gender objectification, and Orientalism are informed by similar cultural processes. These issues, particularly gender, continued to be central in the cultural significance of the *bolero* throughout its history.

ACTIVITY 3.5. *Find one or two poems of Orientalist inspiration by* Modernista *poets (for example, Rubén Darío's "Medallones" or "La negra Dominga"). How do these poems use references to Oriental culture and Otherness? How are women and their bodies portrayed by these poets? Which similarities and differences do you find between the Modernista's approach and that of* bolero *composers like Guty Cárdenas and Luis Rosado Vega?*

MEXICO CITY AND THE PRODUCTION AND POPULARIZATION OF THE MEXICAN *BOLERO*: 1930s–1950s

If the radio, recording, and film industries were fundamental in making Guty Cárdenas into the first Mexican music idol, they also played a central role in the popularization of the *bolero* from the 1930s on. A list of some composers and singers important in the popularization of the musical genre as well as in shaping its appeal as a cosmopolitan urban genre is provided in the companion website. Many of these actors and musicians not only owe much of their fame to the *bolero*, but the genre also owes them its transformation and successful reception as a Mexican genre between the 1930s and 1960s. The talent of this generation of composers and charisma of these interpreters made the *bolero* into Mexico's cosmopolitan urban music within the context of migration from the countryside to the city after the Mexican Revolution.

The foundation of the radio station XEW in 1930 was crucial for the development of a powerful Mexican media industry, changing the face of Mexico's radio industry and playing a central role in the development of Telesistema Mexicano / Televisa, one of the most powerful entertainment networks in Latin America. Its founder, Emilio Azcárraga Vidaurreta, first thought of XEW as a business; this made it different from earlier Mexican radio stations, created as experimental and cultural or educational ventures. XEW, allied with RCA Victor since 1935, devised a marketing strategy to offer entertainment to its audience and prompt new consumerist habits among them. XEW developed this aggressive plan at the crucial moment of Mexico's modern nation-building, thus making the station and its companion entertainment industry into providers of contents that quickly became icons of Mexican modernity. Furthermore, the station's slogan, "La Voz de la América Latina desde México" (the voice of Latin America from Mexico) suggests that Azcárraga Vidaurreta was a visionary entrepreneur interested in creating and exploiting markets beyond the borders of his country. The station attracted the best talent from Mexico and abroad, and soon its singers, actors, and musicians, in alliance with the nascent film and recording industries, became the most visible part of a cultural and marketing project that helped in consolidating a cosmopolitan Latin American popular culture but also threatened local traditions.

ACTIVITY 3.6. *Discuss in class. Could the presence of Mexican cultural products throughout Latin America be considered a type of cultural imperialism? How does cultural imperialism affect the development of local traditions?*

Probably no music expresses better the dynamics at work at the intersection of nation-building, modernization, private entrepreneurship, and their relation to the construction of gender roles and stereotypes in 1930s and 1940s Mexico than the *boleros* of Agustín Lara. Their importance in the formation of radio Mexican audiences and their ubiquitous presence in Mexican films provide an ideal example to explore the relationships between the radio and film industries, the development of cosmopolitan urban sensibilities, and the construction of gender

FIGURE 3.5. *Statue of Agustín Lara in Veracruz. (© Ekaterina Pirozhenko. Used by permission of Ekaterina Pirozhenko, 2012.)*

typologies and relations in mid-20th-century Mexico. Although Agustín Lara composed songs in many different genres, his international reputation is based on his *bolero* production. Called El Flaco de Oro (The Golden Skinny) by his followers, Lara was born in Mexico City. In the mid-1920s he was playing piano at brothels and cabarets in the city; it was there that he composed his first famous *bolero*, "Imposible" (Impossible), inspired by a song by Guty Cárdenas (Dueñas 2005: 25), in 1927. "Imposible" quickly became a hit, recorded by many artists for the Columbia and Brunswick labels, and landed him a contract with Victor. Lara's success made him a natural hire for Azcárraga Vidaurreta's XEW and from 1930 to 1939 Lara hosted *La Hora Íntima,* one of the most successful radio shows of the station, through which he introduced hundreds of his songs to a national audience. Many of these songs were included in films, and a few movies were loosely based on their lyrics. Figure 3.5 shows a statue of Agustín Lara in Veracruz, Mexico.

Lara's musical style was the synthesis of numerous musical influences: Trova Yucateca (especially Cárdenas's *boleros*), the refined character of *Modernista* poetry, the piano style that prevailed among cabaret and brothel musicians (which privileged a slower style that invited couples' sensual dancing), and an erotic imagery that made him the target of moralistic attacks throughout his life. "Imposible" is a good example of Lara's early style. Although Cuban elements such as the accompanying *cinquillo* and clave are still prominent, the lyrics combine the exaltation of female beauty, evident in the Yucatecan style, with a new twist: the nightlife as background and an oblique apology of women forced into prostitution by the social inequalities of modern urban life. If Cárdenas' "Pasión" relishes in the sensual imagery of the unknown and mysterious female body, Lara's "Imposible" focuses on the impossibility of real love between a prostitute and a customer who has fallen in love with her. While she sells her body in a brothel ("cambias tus besos por dinero" [you exchange your kisses for money]), her pursuer recognizes that uncontrollable circumstances have pushed her to this lifestyle and states that only God can judge her actions ("y tu castigo se lo dejo a Dios" [I leave your punishment to God]).

Lara's infatuation with prostitutes reflects a larger cultural obsession in 1930s Mexico. The first Mexican sound film, *Santa* (1931), is the story of a countryside girl who, after being seduced and abandoned by a soldier, is rejected by her family and forced to move to Mexico City and work as a prostitute at a luxurious brothel. This plot or variations of this plot became standard in Mexican cinema throughout the 20th century. It is no coincidence that the film's main song is Lara's *bolero* "Santa," for the music and film both reflected the modern idea that urban life could lead to moral corruption. Lara's songs focus on the impossibility of love or its dramatic impermanence among men and women whose lives were determined by the circumstances of urban life. A good example of how these topics and the gender roles they perform and reproduce were amplified by the relationship between popular music and the film industry is Lara's *bolero* "Aventurera" (Adventuress).

"Aventurera" (CD track 4) offers an interesting form as well as unusual motivic and melodic organization within the conventions of the *bolero* genre. A detailed analysis of structure of "Aventurera" can be found in the companion website. As in "Imposible" and "Santa," the muse in "Aventurera" is a prostitute. However, in this case, the singing voice is not that of an improbable lover but rather of a kind of advisor who, understanding the woman's tragic life ("since the infamy of your cruel destiny / withered your admirable spring"), admonishes her to make the best out of it ("whoever desires the honey in your lips / let them pay for your sin with diamonds"). Like most of Lara's *bolero*'s "Aventurera" is short, condensed, and uncomplicated in its theme, focusing the listener's attention on one sentiment throughout the song. Since the topics are similar and the song's stories simple, one could read or hear them as complementary, as episodes in a larger story about female and male relations in 1930s–1940s post-revolutionary, modernizing, urban Mexico.

ACTIVITY 3.7. *Listen to Agustín Lara's "Aventurera" following the charts and analysis provided in the companion website. Identify the issues explained in the text and discuss in class the main features of the song.*

Although popular, the erotic lyrics in many of Lara's *boleros* encountered strong opposition from Mexico's most conservative sectors, some of his songs being censored as immoral or sacrilegious. Attacked for the lyrics of "Palabras de mujer" (Words of a Woman): "aunque no quieras tu, ni quiera yo, ni quiera Dios" (although you don't want it, although I do not want it, and although God does not want it) his song was interpreted as blasphemous by Catholic authorities since its lyrics implied that human affairs could be conducted against God's will; eventually Lara was forced to change "Ni quiera Dios" to "Lo quiere Dios" (God wants it).

Polemics aside, Lara's *boleros* speak of a modern world that, from a masculine and conservative perspective, seems to spin out of control, particularly in terms of gender relations. Mid-20th-century Mexican modernization was characterized by massive migration from the countryside to the cities, the expansion of the working class, and the growing presence of women in the workforce. *Bolero* lyrics respond to this, showing male fears of losing social control by presenting prostitution as the alternative to the idealized place of "controlled" women as housekeepers. It also shows masculine desires to control and possess women through the over-sexualized female body of the prostitute as the object of love. This was a body males could have access to through money precisely because of women's entrance into the work force.

> **ACTIVITY 3.8.** *Compare the lyrics of Cárdenas' "Pasión" and Lara's "Aventurera" and how these two songwriters represent women. How do you think these different expressions of desire of the female body inform different ideas about gender relations and the place of women in Mexican society?*

The instrumentation of the first recordings of "Aventurera" from the 1930s and 1940s is very different from the contemporary rendition of Los Tres Reyes in the companion CD. These earlier recordings privilege piano and violin ensembles or orchestrations featuring strings, winds, and piano unlike guitar ensembles of the earlier Trova Yucateca tradition. This shift could be interpreted through cosmopolitanism: as Mexican musicians borrowing music, particularly the jazz and big band sounds from the 1930s that were flowing from the United States into Mexican markets. Many transnational recording labels had had a presence in Mexico since the early 20th century and by the 1920s had brought Mexican talent such as Guty Cárdenas and later Tito Guízar, one of the first icons of the mariachi tradition, to the United States to produce recordings for Spanish-speaking audiences. However, the true goal of these labels in Mexico was creating markets for musicians in their catalogue rather than developing a roster of local artists. The permanent establishment of RCA Victor Mexicana in 1935 (in alliance with Azcárraga's radio station XEW) and Columbia in 1947 initiated a more systematic attempt to develop Mexican and Latin American markets. Audiences were eager to consume the latest musical trends from New York and Hollywood, but also wished to hear their local idols. RCA Victor's alliance with XEW allowed it access to a fabulous distribution machine and the radio station's talent, thereby developing a roster of Mexican and Latin American artists to better satisfy the demands of their new markets.

This moment coincided with the establishment of the Roosevelt administration's Good Neighbor policy, based on a new principle of non-interference in Latin American affairs. Instead of the United States' old strategy of military occupation, the Good Neighbor policy aimed to gain Latin American support at the onset of international conflicts, and promoted military aid, political pressure, cultural penetration, and economic alliances with local elites and entrepreneurs. This favored a flourishing entertainment industry in Mexico with strong ties to the

United States resulting in a strong influence of the latter on the former. Thus, the new orchestral sound that began dominating the *bolero* production of composers like Lara, Gonzalo Curiel, and Consuelo Velázquez in the 1930s and 1940s reveals the success in Mexico of the sound of Cole Porter, Bing Crosby, Jimmy Dorsey, Benny Goodman, and Glenn Miller, among others. This type of *bolero* focused on romantic love, disregarding the erotic and racy lyrics for which Lara had been criticized. The continual North/South musical dialogue was also advanced by many musicians, singers, and composers active throughout the Americas. The success of Velázquez, María Grever, and Alberto Domínguez—whose *bolero*s were recorded countless times by major U.S. orchestras such as Goodman's, Dorsey's, and Artie Shaw's, and soloists like Sinatra—and the incorporation of *bolero* elements into the *bolero*-beguine shows the *bolero* as a space that fulfilled the cosmopolitan as well as romantic aspirations of both Latin American and United States audiences.

By the 1930s a Mexican *bolero* style is apparent. Unlike the early Trova Yucateca or the Cuban and Puerto Rican *bolero*, the Mexican style was slower, more harmonically complex, and slowly shed the clave and *cinquillo*, the Afro-Caribbean rhythms that characterized *bolero* styles throughout the Caribbean. The erasure of African elements from the Mexican *bolero* style seemed necessary for the larger racial discourse of *mestizaje* that the country adopted as a national identity. As mentioned in Chapter 1, the notion of *mestizaje* as national identity eschewed Mexico's African heritage to emphasize its indigenous and Spanish past. The development of a unique Mexican *bolero* style, free from obvious African references is a good example of how music and talk about music play a role in the normalization of larger ideological discourses.

TRIOS AND *BOLERO RANCHERO*: THE 1950s AND 1960s

During the 1930s and 1940s, the guitar trio, although less popular than the orchestral *bolero*, was a customary *bolero* ensemble, with Trío Calaveras, Hermanos Flores, and Trío Tariácuri among many active in radio, recordings, and films. However, with the success of Los Panchos, a trio formed in New York in 1948 by Mexican guitarists and composers Chucho Navarro and Alfredo "El Güero" Gil, and its lead singer, Puerto Rican Hernando Avilés, the format became the dominant *bolero*

FIGURE 3.6. *Los Panchos from the film* Perdida *(1950). (Courtesy of Alejandro L. Madrid)*

ensemble in the 1950s (Figure 3.6 shows a picture of Los Panchos from the movie *Perdida*). The ensemble includes two rhythm guitars and a *requinto* (different from *requinto jarocho*, it is a small high-pitched guitar tuned a fourth higher than a regular guitar: A D G C′ E′ A′); some variants replaced one of the rhythm guitars with maracas. The version of "Aventurera" in the accompanying CD (track 4) is performed by Los Tres Reyes. This trio was formed in 1958 by Hernando Avilés and the brothers Raúl and Gilberto Puente, but this recording features the current members of the trio, the Puente brothers and Cuban singer Bebo Cárdenas. It offers a good example of the guitar trio performance style characterized by virtuoso *requinto* solos in the introduction and interludes (played by Gilberto Puente at 0–0:20 and 1:46–2:04), with the solo from the beginning repeated in the interlude.

These solos give trios their distinct sound and musical identity; many solos by Puente and El Güero Gil, two of the best *requinto* players in *bolero* history, can be found in YouTube recorded by fans who imitate them to perfection. *Requinto* solos are based on virtuoso sequences that combine fast scale and arpeggio passages and usually also play a counterpoint to the main vocal line throughout the song. The rhythm guitar plays a simple accompaniment that could be based on the typical *bolero* guitar accompaniment or on more technically complicated arpeggio unfoldings of the song's harmonic changes. Vocal parts are sung in three-part homophony, with a high-pitched lead voice singing the main melody in a luscious, crooner-like style, and the second and third voices providing a harmony via parallel or oblique motion below the main melody. First introduced by Los Panchos, this style was adopted as a performance standard in the 1950s and 1960s by most trios, including Los Tres Reyes.

Trios remained popular until the 1960s providing the medium for many singers to start their solo careers and a venue for a new genera-tion of composers born in the 1920s. This was not the only *bolero* type in 1950s and 1960s Mexico. The increasing acceptance of mariachi and *ranchera* music as a type of national music in earlier decades influenced *bolero* composers who incorporated this genre into the mariachi, giving birth to the *bolero ranchero*. Pablo Dueñas suggests that the *bolero ranchero* was born rather serendipitously in 1949, when the movie star Pedro Infante recorded a mariachi version of "Amorcito corazón" (My Little Love Heart), a song he had recorded earlier with orchestra. The mariachi version of this *bolero* marked the beginning of the *bolero ranchero* (Dueñas 2005: 57); it helped make this a top-selling recording and ignited the career of many singers in the 1950s and 1960s. Following the market-ing strategy that had proved successful in the 1930s these vocalists also attempted movie careers.

Bolero ranchero became a standard genre in the mariachi repertoire and some of Mexico's most important popular musicians have still kept it a popular genre among contemporary listeners. It represents the inter-section of the two musical traditions that came to dominate the musical representation of the country in the 1930s and 1940s through the enter-tainment industry: the *bolero* as the cosmopolitan genre referencing the urban experience of those who migrated to the cities—especially Mexico City—and the mariachi as the ensemble that represented the Mexican countryside as a source of pride, authenticity, and even a machista model of masculinity.

The adoption of the *bolero* by the musical ensemble that had come to represent the quintessential mestizo Mexican music experience helped further eliminate traces of blackness in the Mexican style of the genre. If Lara had slowed the Trova Yucateca *bolero* making it a more sensual dancing experience, and if the orchestral and trio versions had largely gotten rid of the remaining Cuban elements in Lara's *bolero*, it was the *bolero ranchero* that effectively rendered invisible any traces of blackness in the Mexican *bolero* by transforming it into a *ranchera* music in perfect alignment with the national discourse of *mestizaje*. This process of de-racialization was pushed forward by the work of Armando Manzanero and other composers in the late 1960s as the genre developed into the *balada* by the end of the decade.

CHAPTER 4

Balada: Cosmopolitanism and the Mexican Romantic Song in the 1970s

Once, during a visit to a friend's apartment in Havana, Cuba, I had a unique opportunity to witness how Mexico and Mexican music are perceived in other Latin American countries. Throughout our dinner, the upstairs neighbor kept playing José José *baladas* loudly on her stereo system; it was our bad luck that she also decided to sing along with them at the top of her lungs. I asked my host if her neighbor was always like that and she replied: "Oh yes. She just loves Mexican music. It is her favorite." I was fascinated to learn that Cubans would associate Mexican music with the romantic *balada* genre sung by José José. But it made perfect sense. If one was to visit a Mexican household in the 1970s or 1980s, one would have most likely heard all types of *baladas*; from the softly orchestrated songs promoted in TV shows like *Siempre en Domingo* (Always on Sunday) to those played by smaller rock-like band formats heard on the radio by domestic workers. The *balada* was a ubiquitous musical genre in Mexico. It was a genre that reflected and shaped ideas about romantic love as well as notions about gender relations and sentimentality in those two decades and beyond. This chapter seeks to identify how the *balada* genre was developed and disseminated, and how it articulated a variety of mainstream and underground sensibilities and gender relations in Mexico. We will try to understand how the *balada* became one of the most popular musical genres among Mexicans at the end of the 20th century, to the point that Mexican music would be associated with it abroad.

SHIFTING TASTE: FROM *BOLERO* TO *BALADA* IN 1960s AND 1970s MEXICO

In the 1970s, with the arrival of new musical trends from the United States, especially rock and disco, the *bolero* lost appeal with Mexican audiences although the kind of sensibility it articulates remained central in their listening experience. The *balada*, a new genre of love song borrowed musical features from the newest United States and European fads but retained the romantic sensibility that had made the *bolero* a favorite among Latin American audiences through the 1960s. There are two *balada* sub-styles—one aimed at the middle and upper-middle classes, the other largely developed within a working-class milieu. Although musically related, these sub-styles articulate different aspirations and stylistic trajectories.

The middle-class *balada* is characterized by its use of large orchestral arrangements and backup vocal singers in combination with electric guitar, electric bass, and drum set. The arrangement style appealed to the aspirations of refinement of these middle classes and also allowed the media to create a representation of Mexican and Latin American audiences as somehow sophisticated and modern. This sub-style is identified mostly with solo singers (*baladistas*) while the *balada* popularized among working classes is connected to the *grupero* boom and characterized by a less sophisticated instrumentation and an emphasis on *grupos* (bands).

The *balada* genre is characterized by a romantic sentimentality that is often accentuated by an extremely dramatic attitude. So central is this feature that one of the marks of a good *balada* singer is his or her ability to convincingly convey the emotional power of these dramatic moments. Many *balada* singers developed a highly mannered singing style that involved weeping or sighing and indulged in moments of intense emotionalism. This also translated into an orchestration style of wider dynamic range, instrumental crescendos, and loud orchestral tutti reinforcing the singing style by punctuating the emotional character of the lyrics. An important difference between the *balada* and the *bolero* is that *balada* melodies tend to be more repetitive than *bolero* ones. This is part of the genre and it allows for the music to be catchy and quickly stick in the listener's memory.

Armando Manzanero (b. 1935) was central in bringing the *bolero* to its apex in the 1960s and in the development of the *balada* for the middle classes. A Yucatán native, he began working as a piano accompanist, composer, and singer in Mexico City in the late 1950s, with rock 'n' roll's rise and *bolero*'s decline. What made Manzanero a key figure was his ability to move successfully from one musical genre to the other, redefining the borders between them. As a composer, arranger, and accompanist he was comfortable working with the Chilean *bolerista* Lucho Gatica, the Mexican rock 'n' roll and pop singer Angélica María, and the Spanish *baladista* Raphael. The love songs in Manzanero's first recording as a singer, *A mi amor, con mi amor* (1967), have often been referred to as *boleros* or *baladas* interchangeably by fans and critics alike; songs like "Adoro" (I Adore), "Esta tarde vi llover" (This Afternoon I Saw the Rain) or "Te extraño" (I Miss You) show compositional features that link them unmistakably to the bolero tradition in form, dramatic content, and overall sentimentality. However, these songs and their arrangements also show distinct features that might identify them with the nascent *balada* tradition: simplicity of lyrics (absent is the refined vocabulary and elaborate poetic imagery of *Modernista* inspiration of Guty Cárdenas and Agustín Lara); arrangements borrowed from rock 'n' roll (especially the sounds of the electric guitar, electric piano or Hammond organ, and the drum set), and lush, soaring violin sections at climatic moments to match the dramatic content of the lyrics.

ACTIVITY 4.1. *Search the Internet for the original arrangements of "Esperaré," "Somos novios," or "Voy a apagar la luz" by Armando Manzanero. Try to locate the stylistic features mentioned above, compare them to other examples of* bolero *from the 1930s, 1940s and 1950s. Articulate how Manzanero's songs borrow from tradition and innovate at the same time.*

Daniel Party suggests that the *balada* emerged in the 1960s as a "modernized alternative to the by-then-old-fashioned bolero" (2006: 2). As such, the appeal of the *balada* was just as cosmopolitan as that of the *bolero* and transnational in that *balada* producers, composers, arrangers, and singers had no intention of developing any local *balada* sound or style. The music industry did not want Mexican, Argentinean, or Spanish *baladas* but a truly transnational genre that would appeal to the romantic sensibility of audiences throughout the Spanish and Lusophone world. The production practices of *balada* recordings were also international as they involved singers, musicians, and arrangers living in different countries. Some of the most sought-after *balada* producers and arrangers in the 1970s and 1980s, the golden age of the genre, were Spanish and Mexican, while *balada* singers came from all over the Americas and Spain (for a list of *balada* musicians visit the companion website). It was customary that for a given production, the artist, the composer, and the arranger and producers would each be from a different country while the recording could be made in yet another one, with the marketing campaign often starting in Mexico. Although *balada* production was a true international endeavor, Mexico remained central for the *balada* industry due to the influence of Televisa, the powerful TV and entertainment network. Artists in the 1970s and 1980s knew that in order to be successful in Ibero-America they needed to be so first in Mexico. Televisa's power of penetration was unrivaled in Ibero-America, and it provided continental exposure to the artists it supported, a large majority of whom were *balada* singers.

TELEVISA AND THE *BALADA*
FOR THE MIDDLE CLASSES

Televisa started as an entertainment corporation in 1972, with the merging of two Mexican TV companies, Televisión Independiente de México (TIM), and Telesistema Mexicano. The latter, derived from the media network created by Emilio Azcárraga Vidaurreta in the 1930s. Televisa eventually became a media emporium that owned and controlled radio stations, newspapers, publishing houses, open and cable TV channels, and music labels in Mexico and abroad. Its growth came with the creation of new TV shows, the hiring of actors and singers who worked exclusively for the company or its affiliates (a strategy inspired by the Hollywood star system), and the development of a market for their products: *telenovelas* (soap operas), children's shows, and music shows. One cornerstone of Televisa's programming was *Siempre en Domingo*, a five-hour long, weekly music and variety show hosted by Raúl Velasco, which ran from 1969 to 1998. *Siempre en Domingo* and Velasco were powerful forces in shaping the musical taste of many generations of Mexicans. It was the promotion by Televisa through this show, its radio stations, and its influence on the recording industry that made *balada* the most popular musical genre in Mexico in the 1970s and 1980s. Furthermore, the international penetration of Televisa made Velasco's show a central arena for Spanish and Latin American *baladistas* wishing to promote their music throughout the Americas, further accentuating the cosmopolitan appeal of the genre.

Another entrepreneurial move that helped make *balada* a transnational phenomenon was the 1971 creation in Mexico of the Organización de Televisoras Iberoamericanas (OTI), a conglomerate of TV networks from all countries in Ibero-America—with the exception of Cuba. Its goal was to stimulate and promote commercial and artistic ties among the constitutive networks. One of its main events was the Festival de la OTI (OTI Festival), a song competition inspired by the Eurovision Song Contest and lasting from 1971 to 2000. Each country organized its own local OTI competition to select the song and singer to represent it at the international contest. In 1970s Mexico, the OTI Festival was one of the entertainment highlights of the year. Families would gather around TV sets to discuss their favorite songs, their interpretation, the quality of the arrangements, the singers' attire and hairstyles; to explain why the most popular singers or the audience's favorite songs would often lose; or to voice conspiracy theories about how the contest was "fixed." The *balada* was the most popular genre among composers and singers entering the contest in Mexico or elsewhere.

Some of the most popular Mexican *baladistas* participated and in most cases their performance at the OTI festival triggered their popularity and careers. This was the case of José José (b. 1948), the son of an opera singer; he began singing *boleros* and bossa nova before becoming the first Mexican *balada* superstar of the 1970s and 1980s, after placing third at the Festival de la Canción Latina (the forerunner of the OTI Festival) in 1970. His success exemplifies the transnational character of the genre because, though he did not win first prize at the festival, his interpretation of Roberto Cantoral's "El triste" (The Sad One) televised live throughout Latin America, made the song an international hit and him an instant star. A statue of José José in Mexico City is shown in Figure 4.1.

ACTIVITY 4.2. *Search the Internet for José José's performance at the Festival de la Canción Latina. Discuss in class the musical elements that may have made this performance a cult phenomenon among* balada *fans.*

In the early 1970s, José José worked with a team of largely Mexican musicians and producers under contract with RCA Victor, generating a string of top-selling recordings that by decade's end resulted in a contract with a new label that paired him with a team of outstanding Spanish producers, composers, and arrangers: Manuel Alejandro, Camilo Blanes, Juan Carlos Calderón, and Rafael Pérez Botija. This collaboration produced recordings and singles that included hits like "Gavilán o paloma" (Hawk or Dove), "Si me dejas ahora" (If You Leave Me Now), "Preso" (Prisoner), "Lo dudo" (I Doubt It), and "El amor acaba" (Love Ends) among many others that earned the singer more than 200 Golden and Platinum Records between 1970 and 1995.

FIGURE 4.1. *Statue of José José in Mexico City. (Courtesy of Alejandro L. Madrid)*

José José's *baladas* style was characterized by sweeping melodies that made use of his wide vocal range (more than two octaves at the height of his career) and masterful, innovative orchestrations that emphasized the deeply emotional tone of the lyrics. With few exceptions, his *baladas* were dramatic love songs that addressed universal topics such as the impermanence of love, the sadness of lost love, and the inability of living without the loved one. These *baladas* reproduce the preferred subjects of romantic song from all over the world, although the link to the Latin American bolero tradition is very strong and determinant in the development of the genre's affective reception.

The 1970s was a decade of political turmoil in Mexico as well as the rest of Latin America. A generation of politically aware youngsters, inspired by the success of the Cuban revolution, supported leftist agendas throughout the continent and this generated a socially motivated musical movement (see Chapter 7) whose followers strongly criticized the mainstream media and its popular music products. A special target was the *balada*, which was seen as a superficial genre whose simple love lyrics promoted evasion from the harsh political realities of the working classes. However, the *balada* occasionally served as a vehicle for expression of more liberal ideas, although always within the context of bourgeois aspirations and conservative values of the country's political and economic elites. This is the case of some of the *baladas* in competition at Mexico's OTI festival. Songwriter and singer José María Napoleón (b. 1948) entered the contest several times including with two of his most famous songs, "Hombre" (Man) and "Vive" (Live); neither of these won but they are good examples of a type of *balada* that attempted to overcome the superficiality many people associated with the genre. "Vive," presented at the 1976 festival, is an admonition to live and enjoy life fully in the present ("tal vez mañana no tengas tiempo" [maybe tomorrow you will have no time]) while emphasizing an almost "Protestant work ethic" that suggests the path to individual success and fulfillment was hard work ("siembra tu tierra y ponte a trabajar" [sow your land and get to work], "del cielo nada te caerá" [nothing will fall from heaven to you]). The song could also be read as an optimistic pre-NAFTA (North American Free Trade Agreement) anthem celebrating the social values at the core of the Mexican Miracle, the promise that hard work would bring social mobility and a better quality of life. Particularly poignant is the phrase "siembra tu tierra y ponte a trabajar," precisely at a moment when the Mexican Miracle was collapsing under the weight of external debt, currency devaluation, and corruption, increasingly forcing peasants to abandon their agricultural lands in search of jobs and economic opportunities in the cities. As such, Napoleón's "Vive" is a commentary on the values of a Mexico slowly fading away and a defense of dearly held liberal middle-class values that were growing increasingly irrelevant for the poor majority of the country's population.

"Hombre" offers interesting insights into liberal ideas about masculinity in a country where women's successes were still meager. The Mexican masculinity praised in Napoleón's *balada* is quite different from masculine stereotypes glorified in mid-20th-century *ranchera* music or *bolero*. Through the first part of the song, his lyrics speak of a similar work ethic celebrated in "Vive," that "real men" would not expect anything to be given to them by God but would instead work for it ("agradécele mejor que tienes vida y trabajas" [better to thank Him for being alive and being able to work]). The last part of the song offers a clear critique of the type of macho masculinity privileged by mainstream Mexican culture, stating that a "real man" is not one who yells and threatens people "ni el que tiene más mujeres, ni el que bebe más" (nor that who has more women, nor that who drinks more). These *baladas* encourage a more sensitive and sometimes enlightened idea of masculinity, showing how the Mexican middle classes acknowledged the shortcomings of their inherited models of masculinity. This new notion of Mexican masculinity was an important component of the civilized cosmopolitan identity that the Mexican middle classes imagined through and reflected in their favorite music during the 1970s.

ACTIVITY 4.3. *Search the Internet for a performance of Napoleón's "Hombre" (preferably his presentation at the 1977 Mexican OTI Festival). Discuss in class the lyrics of the song as well as Napoleón's performance style.*

BALADA GRUPERA AND WORKING-CLASS SENTIMENTALITY

If the *baladas* supported by Televisa and the Mexican mainstream music entertainment industry reveal the desires and aspirations of the Mexican middle class in the 1970s and 1980s, the *balada* style developed within the *grupero* musical trend speaks about sensibilities and aspirations of the working classes. *Grupero balada* bands usually started their musical career with economic constraints. Instead of expensive productions by famous *balada* arrangers and soloists, they replaced the large orchestrations and backup singers with smaller rock-type formats that included electric guitars, electric bass, drum set, and most important, an electric organ (and later synthesizers). The instrumental format allowed musicians to reduce costs and permitted less-affluent people and organizations to hire them for lower-budget parties and events. This *balada grupera* was music by low-income working-class musicians for low-income working-class people. The musical feature that became one of the most salient trademarks of *balada* bands like Los Bukis, Los Temerarios, or Los Yonics, the screechy timbre, bright sound of the long sustained electric organ chords, was a consequence of these musicians' economic constraints.

The arrival of rock 'n' roll in Mexico in the early 1960s helped create many local *grupos* (bands) with the central repertory being Spanish covers of U.S. hits (see Chapter 7). Although famous groups established musical careers playing exclusively rock 'n' roll and songs made popular by Elvis Presley, the Shirelles, or the Platters, less successful bands began incorporating *boleros* and *baladas* into their repertories to expand their markets. Playing at low budget events in poor neighborhoods in Mexico City, its suburbs, and smaller towns and villages in the countryside, often at events the more famous rock 'n' roll bands avoided, allowed early *balada grupera* bands to develop a faithful working-class fan base.

The huge success in early 1970s Mexico of Los Ángeles Negros was crucial to developing the musical style characteristic of the *balada grupera* sound. Formed in Chile by Chilean and Argentinean musicians, the band combined *bolero* and *balada* with the sound of U.S. and British rock bands from the same period, creating a sound very different from the Televisa-supported *balada* singers. The band's style, based on the Santana-like quality of electric guitar solos, the Manzarek-like sound of the electric organ, and the high-pitched vocals of Germain de la Fuente inspired and became a standard for Mexican *grupos*. One, Los Bukis, from Michoacán in southwestern Mexico, signed a record contract with Discos Melody helping them become the first super star *balada grupera* band on the Mexican music scene. Los Bukis's early style remained influenced by the electric-organ sound of Los Ángeles Negros but slowly changed as the band became more successful. In keeping pace with technological innovation, the band shifted from the electric organ to the Roland synthesizer and added electronic percussion that provided a larger timbric and rhythmic palette for their arrangements. Although not a type of dance music band per se, Los Bukis incorporated elements from *cumbia*; "Tu cárcel" (Your Jail) and "Y ahora te vas" (Now You Leave), two of the band's most representative songs, reaching numbers 3 and 1 in the charts in 1987 and 1988, respectively, are good examples of the simple love lyrics that characterized their songs and the rhythmic drive borrowed from *cumbia*.

In the 1980s, many Mexican groups followed Los Bukis, developing a sound that combined *cumbia* and *balada*; Los Temerarios and Los Yonics were among the most popular. With their success in the Mexican countryside and among Mexican communities in the United States, the collapse of the Mexican Miracle, and the shrinking of the middle class, the mainstream music industry in Mexico City realized the economic potential of the largely neglected working-class market and accepted its favorite musics, popularizing them via alternative music networks. Televisa featured *onda grupera* bands, especially on its premier music show *Siempre en Domingo*. Until the 1980s, *Siempre en Domingo* privileged sophisticated *balada* for the middle and upper classes, part of a larger tacit cultural project attempting to represent Mexico as a modern, urbane society. The *grupero balada* challenged this endeavor. Furthermore, the mainstream

FIGURE 4.2.   *Los Bukis performing in* Siempre en Domingo *in 1977. (Courtesy of Alejandro L. Madrid)*

balada, with its large symphonic arrangements, had erased the traces of African culture that were still present in older Mexican romantic genres; the association of the *balada grupera* to the *onda grupera* trend and its *cumbia* sound, also challenged the representation of Mexico as a country without African heritage. Figure 4.2 shows Los Bukis performing on Raúl Velasco's show *Siempre en Domingo*.

The *grupero* bands knew their fan base and in their lyrics exhibit a working-class sensibility that often celebrated poverty as a symbol of goodness and authenticity. In Los Bukis' "Tu cárcel," Los Yonics' "Pero te vas a arrepentir" (But You Will Regret It), and Los Temerarios' "Pobre tonto enamorado" (Poor In-Love Fool), this kind of rhetorical turn identifies those rejected or abandoned by their lovers for being poor ("Pobre tonto que te ofrecía lo poco que él tenía" [Poor fool who offered you the little things he had] in "Pobre tonto enamorado") and whose true feelings were never properly appreciated ("Tu vanidad no te deja entender que en la pobreza se sabe querer" [Your vanity does not let you see that in poverty one truly knows how to love] in "Tu cárcel"). The abandoned subject advises a former lover that money will not bring the happiness that sincere love guaranteed ("No es nada su riqueza comparada con lo que a tí te dí" [Wealth is nothing compared to what I gave you] in "Pero te vas a arrepentir"), and warns that (s)he will never again experience true love ("Mil cosas mejores tendrás pero un cariño sincero jamás" [You will have a thousand better things but never a sincere love] in "Tu cárcel"). The plot in these songs is a convention that offers rhetorical vindication to working-class consumers through the listening and sharing of *balada* music affirming that, despite their poverty, they have something more valuable than wealth: sincere, authentic feelings not "corrupted" by money.

Since the economic model and the state failed to provide means for social mobility for the Mexican working classes, these symbolic constructions allowed individuals to believe in a sense of worthiness despite their oppressed conditions. The working-class *balada* shows perfectly how music could be an instrument of social control, a space for individual sublimation, and a response to the desires and aspirations of modernity and cosmopolitanism that mainstream *baladas* articulated. This was also an international sub-style, for many of the bands that played at low-budget countryside events along with the most popular Mexican groups came from South America, including Los Pasteles Verdes from Peru, Los Terrícolas from Venezuela, and Los Bríos from Argentina. In these countries this music was associated with a similar working-class sensibility, often disparaged by the middle and upper classes as unsophisticated and a marker of bad taste, the music of domestic workers (mostly female) who patronized these bands' concerts. The issues of class that determine the reception of this music show *balada* to be contentious, a space where issues of distinction and difference could be negotiated and reinforced.

ACTIVITY 4.4. *Search the Internet for videos of some of the songs by Los Terrícolas, Los Ángeles Negros, Los Bukis, or Los Yonics discussed in the text. Compare their musical and performance style; make comparative charts addressing dressing codes, body movement on the stage, the histrionics of singing, and other elements that may grab your attention.*

MASCULINE, FEMININE, AND QUEER SENSIBILITIES IN THE *BALADA*

Canciones de amor y contra ellas (Songs of love and against women) is the epithet many Mexicans use to identify the type of sensibility that permeates many *boleros* and *baladas* as well as *ranchera* songs, the lyrics presenting a scenario in which a woman leaves a man whose sincere love she was not able to truly appreciate. Although many of these lyrics are gender neutral, the audience tends to hear them as the expression of male desires and anxieties toward the female because most composers of *balada* are men. Indeed, these *balada* songs often reproduce the patriarchal views on gender of the *bolero* (with exceptions such as José María Napoleón's "Hombre").

However, the *balada* also expresses an extremely sensitive and vulnerable masculinity only hinted at in previous romantic song genres. In traditional *boleros*, the male's voice is somehow in control regardless of singing the role of an abandoned lover; however, in the *balada*, the male character is allowed to express his sadness in affected and often exaggerated gestures that define the genre's dramatic effect. A good example of how *balada* masculine sentimentality challenges the type of machista masculinity privileged in popular culture through the 1960s is King Clave's "Los hombres no deben llorar" (Men Should Not Cry), whose commercial success in Mexico opened the doors of *Siempre en Domingo* to its Argentinean songwriter. The male character publicly acknowledges that, despite the common view that men should never cry, he cannot control his sadness upon discovering his lover's betrayal. This song's dramatic sentimentality is shared by many *baladas* and is an example of how the genre allows for the expression of forbidden or repressed aspects of masculinity within a largely patriarchal and chauvinist system of gender relations. According to Brazilian musicologist Martha Tupinambá de Ulhôa, the type of masculine vulnerability and victimization that characterizes *baladas*, which arguably appeals to the singers' large female fan base, is a strategy to symbolically penetrate the domestic sphere and "engage in romance" while still maintaining the public sphere as a male domain (Ulhôa quoted in Party 2006: 9).

An even more interesting case in relation to the *balada* as a space for the expression of a type of masculine vulnerability not seen in previous love song genres is that of Juan Gabriel (b. 1950). Winner of Billboard, Grammy, Latin Grammy, and MTV awards, he is in possession of more than 1,500 Golden, Platinum, and Multi-Platinum Records and is arguably the most successful Mexican singer, songwriter, and producer of the last three decades of the 20th century. Juan Gabriel's contributions to the *balada* repertory include classics like "Busca un amor" (Search for a Love), "He venido a pedirte perdón" (I Came to Ask for Your Forgiveness), "Querida" (Dear),"Siempre en mi mente" (Always in My Mind), and "Yo no nací para amar" (I Was Not Born to Love). Early in his career when he achieved fame as a *balada* singer and composer, Juan Gabriel was portrayed as a young, overly sensitive man, an authentic artist at heart. Such persona is emphasized in his 1982 biopic *Es mi vida* (*It Is My Life*), as well as earlier films *En esta primavera* (*In This Spring*) (1979) and *El Noa Noa* (1980), where he plays the same simple, extremely well-mannered, good, noble, and sensitive man. Audiences transferred the attributes of Juan Gabriel's characters in the films to him and immediately empathized with him.

The vulnerability of the *balada* musical persona allowed Juan Gabriel to express through it his own homosexual identity without much animosity from the largely homophobic Mexican society of the 1970s (gay rights organizations became more visible and influential only in the 1980s). Although never publicly accepted, his homosexuality is an open secret that has not affected his career negatively; instead, he and his public persona have thrived among both female and heterosexual male audiences. Reportedly, male audiences at his *palenque* (countryside cock fight arenas often used for music performances) concerts would go crazy over his gay mannerisms and body language; something he often exaggerated as the audience expected it from him.

Some of Juan Gabriel's early hits attain a new significance when interpreted within a queer sensibility that takes into account the composer's alleged sexual identity. "Yo no nací para amar," a catchy and dramatic melody, follows the conventions of the *balada* in its neutral presentation of the object of love, easily read within a heterosexual framework as another heartbreak story of a man who witnesses how, as his childhood friends grow older and find lovers, he is unable to find true love. In the climax of the song Juan Gabriel answers his friends' concerns about his loneliness with the dramatic cry that gives its song its title "Yo no nací para amar, nadie nació para mí, tan solo fuí un loco soñador nomás…mis sueños nunca se volvieron realidad" (I was not born to love, nobody was born for me; I was just a crazy dreamer, no more…my dreams never came true). What seems like a dramatic confession about a sad and loveless life acquires new meaning when read through a gay lens. Thus, "Yo no nací para amar, nadie nació para mí" is no longer an explanation or pathetic cry that demands our compassion but rather a façade, an alibi within the heteronormative structure, that hides the deeper and more complex structural reason for his loneliness (or apparent loneliness). It is this very oppressive heteronormative structure that creates the conditions for his or her dreams never to come true and for his or her life to be "sadder and darker every day" as society denies homosexual individuals the same right to happiness that heterosexual couples take for granted. In this context, it is not that the character in the song was not born to love but that his or her love is not recognized as such within the mainstream repressive heteronormative system and a relationship is therefore discouraged or rendered socially invisible. In both cases, this ends with the absence of a partner from the opposite sex, and in the heteronormative system this is a social deficiency that needs to be explained.

ACTIVITY 4.5.   *Search the Internet for one of Juan Gabriel's performances of "Yo no nací para amar" (preferably from early in his career). Analyze the singer's performance style in relation to the lyrics. Pay attention to the body language and gestures he uses to convey the emotional content of the song.*

Another case of queer sensibility expressed through the *balada* is that of singer and songwriter Ana Gabriel (b. 1955). Born María Guadalupe Araujo Yong, the granddaughter of a Chinese immigrant, she started her music career in 1977 and participated in the national OTI festival, which, unlike many famous male *baladistas*, she won as songwriter and singer in 1987. This was a turning point in her career and helped her transition from a modest artist into arguably the most successful Mexican female singer/songwriter since Lolita de la Colina (b. 1948), one of the most prolific Mexican female songwriters from the earlier generation of *baladistas*. As with Juan Gabriel, Ana Gabriel's homosexuality is an open secret that she has never publicly verified. However, the artist has a large and faithful gay fan base that she consciously nurtures, and she acknowledges having written one of her most popular songs, "Simplemente amigos" (Simply Friends) for them. Figure 4.3 shows Ana Gabriel.

As in Juan Gabriel's "Yo no nací para amar," the homosexual experience that informs "Simplemente amigos" is disguised within the parameters of heterosexual love; the subject of love is kept neutral in the song's lyrics and in the song's official video, where Ana Gabriel narrates a heterosexual love story. This strategy makes the song simply about a secret love. The reasons this relationship may be forbidden are never revealed; the lyrics only inform the listener that in their everyday life the characters of the story pretend to be just friends ("ante la gente es así; amigos, simplemente amigos") (before everybody it is like this; friends, simply friends). But the lyrics also inform us that a clandestine relationship takes place behind closed doors ("¿pero quién sabe en realidad lo que sucede entre los dos?") (but who really knows what happens between the two

FIGURE 4.3.   *Ana Gabriel singing at the 1987 OTI Festival. (Courtesy of Alejandro L. Madrid)*

of us?). Moreover, the lyrics also emphasize the characters' frustration at having to keep their love secret ("cuanto daría por gritarles nuestro amor") (how much would I give to scream about our love). Once the song is read against the background of the homosexual experience that inspired it, as acknowledged by Ana Gabriel, the plot changes radically; it becomes a song that speaks about the painful double life that homosexuals are forced to live in a largely homophobic society.

ACTIVITY 4.6. *Search the Internet for the official video of Ana Gabriel's "Simplemente amigos." Analyze the relationship between images and lyrics taking under consideration the composer's acknowledgment that the song was written for her gay fans.*

While a large majority of *balada* singers, composers, and arrangers are men, women have managed to succeed as *baladistas*—although often, their songs and musical personae uncritically reproduce patriarchal hierarchies. However, Lolita de la Colina and Lupita D'Alessio

(b. 1954) are noteworthy in this regard because they challenged this male-dominated system. Songwriter Lolita de la Colina's career began in the 1970s; she is one of the most prolific Mexican songwriters, having composed songs for some of the most famous male and female *balada* singers. De la Colina achieved fame for her racy lyrics, which were shocking for the conservative middle-class *balada* consumers of the 1970s. Her most notorious songs resulted from her collaboration with singer Lupita D'Alessio and were central in shaping the musical persona of the singer as La Leona Dormida (The Sleeping Lioness)—a strong-willed woman reacting against controlling men and asserting women's right to their own sexual pleasure.

De la Colina's songs translated into music D'Alessio's personal experience as she endured the public process of divorce from her first husband, Jorge Vargas, an unexceptional *balada* and *ranchera* singer who had achieved some success in the mid-1970s. The media of the time suggested that Vargas wanted D'Alessio to assume a more traditional housewife role and felt threatened by her success. True or not, it became a cornerstone for the development of D'Alessio's new public persona as an independent woman ready to criticize the inadequacies of lovers as controlling men. Lolita de la Colina's songs, direct and scandalously erotic on occasions, were fundamental in solidifying this representation. "Ya no regreso contigo" (I Will Not Go Back to You) and "Punto y coma" (Semicolon) are good examples of the fruitful collaboration between the two women; these songs embody the harsh and often sarcastic, critical stance against men for which D'Alessio would become famous. An influential feminist movement developed in Mexico in the aftermath of the challenging leftist student protests that shook Mexican society in 1968 (see chapter 7). D'Alessio and de la Colina's songs resonated with women becoming aware of the persistence of gender inequalities and the sexism permeating Mexican society. For many, these songs became unofficial anthems against male domination in both private and public life.

> **ACTIVITY 4.7.** *The erotic quality of many of the* baladas *written to empower a female's right to sexual pleasure beyond male control tended to reproduce old stereotypes of women as sexualized objects. Organize with your classmates a class debate upon the following questions: Are these songwriters' and singers' strategies successful in developing an awareness of gender inequalities in male-dominated societies? What contradictions does such strategy raise? Do you find similar cases among U.S. singers?*

Romantic songs like the *balada* and its predecessor, the *bolero*, are music genres that demand deeply emotional and sometimes even dramatic responses from their fans. Looking at them closely, with a critical eye, helps us understand the wide variety of social discourses they articulate. It is particularly clear how, by engaging the way in which couples relate to each other, often reflecting on the power struggles that inform the dynamics between lovers, love songs are windows into the way gender is performed in society. The *balada* and its consumption in Mexico offer an opportunity to reflect on these issues.

CHAPTER 5

Norteña Music and Its History of Hybridization

My fondest memories as a child growing up in the north of Mexico inevitably include the anticipated weekly gatherings with friends or relatives. These get-togethers were more or less the same every time; the men lit the fire and grilled *the carne asada* (grilled meat) in the yard while the women prepared the *tortillas de harina* (wheat tortillas) and drinks in the kitchen. The best part came later, when *norteña* music was played; kids would dance on a wooden door used as *tarima* and adults would tirelessly talk about the lyrics of the *corridos*, trying to unmask the identities of the characters and towns mentioned in the songs. Today, I realize that these gatherings were celebrations of *norteño* identity; from the *tortillas de harina* to the *norteña* music, they were all cultural goods that made my family and friends different from other Mexicans. Especially the music; *norteña* was a type of accordion-driven music that I never heard when I went to my cousins' houses in Mexico City or Veracruz. Back then, in the early 1970s, *norteña* music was very localized, popular in the north of Mexico but with exceptions, largely unknown in the rest of the country. It was only in the 1990s that *norteña* music became ubiquitous in the Mexican media as part of the so-called *Onda Grupera* (Bands Craze). Remembering the uniqueness of *norteña* identity when I was a child leads me to ask myself how a marker of local identity like *norteña* music, which had been neglected by mainstream Mexican culture for decades, could become central to Mexican musical identity at the beginning of the 21st century. And also, why was its reception in the rest of the country engulfed within the label *Onda Grupera*? This chapter traces the development of this music tradition and advances some answers to these questions.

THE MYTH OF *ONDA GRUPERA*

In the 1990s, *Onda Grupera* came to dominate the Mexican music industry. The term identified a wide range of musical practices that had little in common other than having been developed and popularized on the margins of the mainstream music industry. The label lumped together *música norteña, banda, cumbia*, their sub-styles, and various new hybrids created by their stylistic cross fertilization. All had their roots in rural Mexico (except *cumbia*) or were favored by the Mexican lower classes and until the 1990s had minimal presence in the mainstream Mexican media.

However, during this decade, radical changes to Mexico's entertainment industry altered Mexico's cultural landscape in important ways; these changes resulted from larger financial vicissitudes due partly to the signing of NAFTA and the economic success of Mexican immigrants in the United States. Immigrants' remittances helped to slowly transform their native rural towns and villages; and the music they embraced, especially *norteña* and *banda* musics—which were also favored by Mexicans and Mexican Americans in the United States—was adopted by their relatives at home. Townspeople in Michoacán, Guerrero, Oaxaca, or Veracruz, where these musics had been largely unknown until the 1970s, adopted them almost as symbols of their immigrant relatives' economic success.

By the late 1990s, the cowboy outfit that characterizes *norteña* and *banda* musicians and fans became pervasive in Mexican TV, also being adopted by many former *balada* composers and singers who joined the *Onda Grupera* craze in an attempt to revive their musical careers. The appearance of *norteño, banda*, and *cumbia* musicians en masse in Mexican TV shows led to the reorganization of the TV-based entertainment industry. Televisa's new infrastructure included magazines and special music awards (Furia Musical), TV shows featuring new Mexican stars and *grupos* (bands), alliances with local, regional, and international (especially from the United States) music labels with long-established distribution networks to produce this music.

The *Onda Grupera* label was born as an overarching, all-embracing marketing term to include all of these formerly marginal styles and genres. It emphasized the fact that these musics were all played by bands although it did not stress the diversity of ensembles, their stylistic unique instrumental features, and the different musical traditions to which they belonged. *Norteña, banda*, and *cumbia* denote different musical typologies; *norteña* and *banda* referring to particular performance styles (that include many musical genres), *cumbia* to a specific musical genre. Therefore many genres could be played in *norteña* and *banda* style, including *corridos, huapangos*, waltzes, polkas, and even *cumbia*— although *cumbia* is generally placed in a different sub-category because it is associated with the performance style of *conjuntos tropicales* (tropical music bands) and developed independently from *banda* and *norteña*. The arrival of *Onda Grupera* into the Mexican entertainment industry coincided with the solidification of a new category in the U.S. Latino music industry, the so-called Regional Mexican music. In the 1980s, the increasingly large Latino population of the United States forced its music industry to recognize the importance of a previously fragmented Latino music market. Los Angeles, New York, San Antonio, and Miami had been the headquarters of the Mexican American, Puerto Rican, Tejano, and Cuban American music industries. Recognition of the purchasing power of different Latino communities occurred when the music industry in general was undergoing major changes and consolidation, with five major recording companies (SONY, EMI, Warner, Universal, and BMG) absorbing most independent labels. In the 1990s, these companies developed Latino music divisions that eventually settled in Miami in an attempt to engage music markets throughout the Americas and consolidate the United States' many Latino music markets into a single one. They created three music categories for this new all-embracing "Latino market": Afro-Caribbean (including Cuban, Puerto Rican, and Dominican genres like salsa, *merengue*, and *bachata*); Latin rock and pop; and Regional Mexican, an umbrella term encompassing all musics with roots in rural Mexico, including mariachi, *ranchera*, *norteña*, *banda*, and even Tejano music.

Cuban American producers were prominent in Miami, and Afro-Caribbean musics had entered the United States mainstream music industry with the introduction of Latin jazz; therefore, the initial marketing emphasis of the Latino music industry was on these genres. This generated animosities between Mexican and Cuban American musicians throughout the 1990s, the former feeling marginalized despite Regional Mexican music outselling all other Latino music genres. In 2000, arguing a bias against Regional Mexican music, Fonovisa, the largest Latino independent music label in the United States at the time, boycotted the first Latino Grammy ceremony, as did nominated Mexican artists like Los Tigres del Norte and Pepe Aguilar. Quickly the United States Latino entertainment industry recognized the growing, influential consumer power of Mexicans (65 percent of the Latino population of the country, spreading beyond their traditional geographic base in the American Southwest into most agricultural areas of the country) (Pacini Hernández 2010: 150). As in Mexico, the huge commercial success of Regional Mexican music changed the mainstream U.S. Latino entertainment industry (despite still being considered unsophisticated and distasteful by upper-class Latinos). The trajectory of *Onda Grupera* in Mexico and Regional Mexican music in the United States should be understood not as parallel phenomena but as aspects of the same transnational complex inclusive of the same musicians and followers, interconnected networks of distribution, and interrelated practices of consumption.

Nevertheless, it is vital to untangle the marketing clutter known as *Onda Grupera* in order to understand how some of the musics marketed under the same label have become meaningful to diverse audiences at different moments in Mexican and Mexican American history. This will enable a better understanding of how their growing interpenetration in a transnational context has generated new, strikingly original hybrid music genres.

ACCORDION MUSIC FROM THE MEXICAN NORTHEAST TO THE WORLD

Un, dos, tres, cuatro (one, two, three, four), the lead singer establishes the beat and the button accordion enters with a syncopated solo in parallel thirds over a typical oom-pah, oom-pah rhythmic base provided by an electric bass that plays on the down beat, and a bajo sexto strumming chords on the upbeat with support from the drum set. The five musicians on stage, wearing stylish white outfits, are showered by green, white, and red lights resembling the hologram of a Mexican flag; flashing light panels in the background and wisps of fog in the foreground provide an almost modernist atmosphere that gives new meaning to the rural musical gestures recognizable in the song's style. This is the concert's climax and the crowd, absorbed by the performance, clap, whistle, and sing along through the first couple of verses before the lead singer utters the end of the second verse, "soy extranjero en mi tierra y no vengo a darles guerra, soy hombre trabajador" (I am a foreigner in my own land, and I did not come to make any troubles, I am a working man), and a loud approving roar from the audience overcomes the theater. The moment is typical of the deep connection between Los Tigres del Norte and their audience created by powerful emotional reactions to the band's music and solidarity with its denunciation of the abuses and discrimination Mexican immigrants suffer in the United States. Los Tigres del Norte's music is an audible space for its fans to proudly reclaim and celebrate their rural origins as well as their rights in their new country. Figure 5.1 shows Los Tigres del Norte during a TV performance.

The song, "Somos más americanos" (We Are More Americans), is a *corrido* in *norteño* style and shows why this music has been meaningful

FIGURE 5.1. *Los Tigres del Norte performing live at the 2008 Latin Grammy Awards. (Courtesy of Alejandro L. Madrid)*

for Mexicans and Mexican Americans for more than a hundred years. The song speaks of the alienation felt by many Mexican immigrants in the United States with xenophobic and racist propaganda accusing them of abusing the immigration and social security systems. Los Tigres del Norte replies to this rhetoric stating that Mexicans immigrated not to create problems but to work hard ("no vengo a darles guerra, soy hombre trabajador"). They also remind the audience that the Southwest has been Mexican territory ("soy extranjero en mi tierra") thus making Mexicans part of the "American" dream, arguably even "more American" than "anglos" as they have been here longer. The song reflects on the notion of transnational belonging that characterizes the experience of the audiences who have embraced this music throughout northern Mexico and the Southwest. It also suggests that *norteña* music has come to represent this migrant culture, articulating the deep feelings of identification that have helped it gain popularity throughout the Mexican diaspora.

In the 2009 PBS documentary *Latino Music USA*, Los Tigres del Norte was called "the most famous band mainstream America never heard of"; indeed they are the most commercially successful band among Latinos in the United States. However, Regional Mexican has marginal status music in the mainstream United States entertainment industry due to its stigma as unsophisticated music and the fact that it is sung in Spanish. How was this music born and how did it become immensely popular throughout the Mexican diaspora and beyond?

Norteña music came to northern Mexico and southern Texas in the late 19th century with the Germans, Czechs, and Poles who settled there after building railroads between Monterrey and Texas in 1882. They introduced the accordion and musical genres like the polka, redowa, and schottische (called *polca, redova,* and *chotís* in northern Mexico) and brought crafts and businesses, like breweries and steel-making, that still define the industrial identity of the Mexican northeast and its long-standing cultural ties with southern Texas. These businesses flourished in Monterrey, just 150 miles south of the Texas border making Monterrey an axis of a commercial and economic network that included Laredo in Texas' Rio Grande Valley, and San Antonio.

This transnational economic circuit was also fundamental in the development of the *norteña* and conjunto musics that came to identify these regions musically during the 20th century. Both musical traditions share a standard instrumentation that includes the button accordion, the *bajo sexto* (a double-stringed bass guitar), the *tololoche* (bass), and the *redova* (a home-made drum now largely replaced by the *tarola* (snare drum) or drum set. Both developed from a core repertory of *polcas, redovas, valses,* and *chotíses* to which local genres such as the *corrido* (a type of descriptive ballad) and *huapango* were added. *Norteño* and conjunto are nearly identical styles, with minor singing and instrumental differences, and named for the regions where they were adopted; *norteña* for the tradition of those living south of the Rio Grande, while conjunto is the term preferred by Mexican Americans and Tejanos. Their history is one of continual dialogue in which performance styles and repertories fluidly move back and forth over the border.

The arrival of polka, redowa, waltz, and schottische to Monterrey and south Texas was part of a larger dance craze for fashionable dances that brought a sense of cosmopolitanism to the urban centers that adopted them in Mexico and the United States during the second part of the 19th century. This was especially important in Mexico as pressures to Europeanize increased among the country's elite; eventually, the same sense of cosmopolitanism caused adoption of those dances in the countryside as symbols of sophisticated European culture. By the 1890s and 1900s the new musical genres were already part of the repertory of more traditionally local music ensembles such as military bands, *orquestas típicas* (string ensembles), and *tamborileros* typical of the Tamaulipas region—also known as *la picota* and formed by clarinets and a homemade drum called *tambora de rancho* (ranch's drum). Local musicians slowly incorporated one- and two-row button accordions, the *bajo sexto*, and the *tambora de rancho* into their ensembles as it was more economical to hire one accordionist than larger orchestral ensembles. By the 1920s, the accordion and *bajo sexto* became the preferred basic instrumental ensemble with occasional additions of *tololoche* and *redova* or *tambora de rancho*. These dance and music traditions traveled with the farming workers throughout Nuevo León, Tamaulipas and south Texas frequently coming into contact with German and Czech communities from whom repertory was borrowed. Many of today's classic *polcas* from the *norteña* and conjunto repertory are in fact German or Czech polkas, such as "El barrilito" (the German "Beer Barrel Polka"). Mexican and Mexican American musicians acknowledge the origins but note that, regardless of their origin, the dances acquire new life and meaning when played by *norteño* and conjunto ensembles.

ACTIVITY 5.1.   *Search the Internet for videos of "Beer Barrel Polka" played by Norwegian American accordionist Myron Floren and "El barrilito" played by Mexican American accordionist Tony de la Rosa. Identify the stylistic differences. How are the European or Anglo and Mexican performances different? Pay attention to the musicians' delivery of the melody, vibrato, use of tempi, rhythmic liberties, syncopation, and improvisation, as well as the different instrumentation and the possibilities they offer. How do these musical elements vary from performance to performance, and how are the musicians able to instill a different feel to their versions? You can find additional material about the differences between the two styles in the following NPR website www.honkytonks.org/ showpages/accordion.htm.*

The standard *norteña* ensemble uses a button accordion, *bajo sexto*, and *tololoche* as its basic instrumental lineup; larger ensembles might use these instruments as the foundation upon which to add clarinets, saxophones, and percussion. The accordion gives the style its characteristic timbre and while most accordion players today play chromatic accordions, some of the earliest great accordionists in the tradition, such as Narciso Martínez, used the diatonic button accordion early in their career. Depending on its type, the instrument would have two to five rows of buttons to play melodic lines with the right hand; the left hand plays harmonies on a buttonboard that has columns of buttons organized by circle of fifths, each button sounding a complete triad. This is the standard left-hand button system called Stardella; more modern button accordions offer more flexibility and freedom to play bass lines and choose the pitches in the harmony. In purely instrumental pieces, the accordion carries the melody; in other songs it would play solos at the beginning and in the middle of the piece; during the rest of the song it provides a fast, arpeggiated harmonic background to the singer. The accordion also plays the embellished cadences that characterize the sectional endings in this style.

The *bajo sexto* is a guitar-like instrument with six double courses; it is tuned by fourths, E-A-D-G-F-C (one octave below the register of the standard guitar), it reinforces the accordion's harmonies, and also plays melodic counterpoints to the vocal part or solo accordion during the improvisatory passages. The *tololoche* is a double bass-like instrument although slightly smaller in size. It may have four strings—although three-string instruments are not unusual—tuned also in fourths, ADGC, one whole step higher than the standard double bass. The *tololoche*, played always in pizzicato style, became part of the standard *norteño* outline in the 1940s and it is still heard in street musician ensembles, although the electric bass has replaced it in more commercial bands. Early *norteño* groups used a percussion instrument called *redova*, a small wooden tablet played with wooden mallets, later replaced by the *tarola* or snare drum, which was replaced by the drum set in contemporary commercial ensembles. Nevertheless, the *redova* can still be heard in traditional, *folklórico* events, and the *tarola* among street and restaurant musicians.

Genres in the core *norteña* repertory include the *polca*, *redova*, *vals*, and *chotís*, all instrumental dances of European origin transformed by their contact with more traditional Mexican genres. The *polca* is a fast dance in simple duple meter (2/4), its rhythmic accompaniment often identified as *oom-pah oom-pah*, an onomatopoeia referring to the bass-chord sequence that characterizes the music (Figure 5.2).

While the phrasing in European polkas tends to emphasize the downbeat, the Mexican *polca* tends to privilege more syncopation, often anticipating the downbeat. Emphasis on the upbeat in Mexican *polca* is also evident in the style of the *bajo sexto*, which regularly plays chords only on the upbeat.

The *redova* and the *vals* are dances in simple triple meter (3/4). Musically they are almost undistinguishable; the dance steps make

FIGURE. 5.2.   *Basic* polca *accompaniment.*

FIGURE 5.3.   *Basic* redova *and* vals *accompaniment.*

FIGURE 5.4.   *Basic* chotís *accompaniment.*

them different, and the dances are what people usually call *oom-pah-pah* (Figure 5.3). The *chotís* is a dance in simple duple meter (2/4 or 4/4) characterized by a basic rhythmic pattern of bass-chord-bass-chord, bass-chord-chord, with all the figures being eighth notes with the exception of the last chord, which is a quarter note (Figure 5.4).

To develop the core *norteña* music repertory, these largely instrumental dance genres combined with some of the local vocal genres, especially the *corrido, ranchera,* and *huapango,* possibly due to the common rhythmic elements and patterns shared among them. Thus, the *corrido norteño,* with its fast simple duple meter alternation of bass and chord fuses the *polca* with the traditional *corrido,* while the simple triple meter of the *redova* and *vals* coincide with the *ranchera* rhythmic pattern, so that *corridos* and *rancheras* in *norteña* style resemble sung *polcas, redovas,* or *valses.* Although the core repertory of *norteña* and conjunto was established in the 1940s and 1950s, the *norteña* musicians' ability to respond to their audience tastes and incorporate the newest musical fads (from *danzón* and *bolero* to *cumbia*) has allowed the tradition's endurance and ability to reinvent itself even into the 21st century.

Narciso Martínez, a native of Reynosa (Tamaulipas) who lived in San Benito, Texas, made the first of many recordings of the type of music that came to be known as *norteña* or conjunto for the Bluebird label, a subsidiary of RCA/Victor, in 1936. Martínez's recordings featured his own compositions in *polca*, *redova*, and *vals* styles played on button accordion and *bajo sexto*. Martínez on accordion and Santiago Almeida on *bajo sexto* made these records, and Cathy Ragland argues that this established the duo as the basic *norteña* ensemble, replacing earlier instrumental ensembles that offered different combinations of the instruments included in *tamborileros* and *orquesta típica* ensembles with or without accordion. Ragland explains that Martínez's unique style came from "playing polkas with the feeling of the shifting rhythm of the *huapango*" which allowed the musicians to move flexibly in and out of the songs' structure to explore melodic, rhythmic, and harmonic variants (2009: 53).

Although Bluebird and RCA/Victor stopped producing recordings in the Rio Grande Valley in 1940, the existing market was taken over by local labels after WWII, the most prominent being Falcon Records and Ideal Records. The first, founded in 1946 by Mexican Americans in the United States, recorded younger accordion players who continued Martínez's *norteña*/conjunto style, among them Valerio Longoria, Tony de la Rosa, and Paulino Bernal. They were the Mexican American accordion players who gave the conjunto style the sound that made it different from *norteña* by incorporating elements from Cajun, country, bluegrass, and other United States folk styles.

In 1948, Los Alegres de Terán, a Mexican duo from General Terán (Nuevo León) that traveled back and forth across the border, made its first recording for Falcon, a label founded in 1947 by Arnaldo Ramírez, a Reynosa native who had worked as disk jockey for a U.S. radio station. Unlike Ideal, which focused on the Mexican American market, Falcon Records developed a roster of Mexican and Mexican American musicians marketed on both sides of the border. Los Alegres de Terán was the label's most famous artist; the group was formed by accordionist Eugenio Ábrego and *bajo sexto* player Tomás Ortiz. Their style cemented the *norteña* as a separate tradition with a sound based on the accordion, *bajo sexto*, and *tololoche*, and a complex vocal style modeled after *bolero* trios like Los Panchos. Before Los Alegres de Terán, singing was rare within the *norteño* tradition; the duo was the first to make singing an integral part of the style and therefore were instrumental in the adoption of *corridos* as a central genre in the repertory of *norteña* musicians, the dominant one among them after the 1970s. Before the success of this generation of musicians in the 1950s, *norteña* and conjunto were considered one and the same tradition; after them, *norteña* came to be identified with Mexicans south of the Rio Grande and conjunto with Mexican Americans in south Texas. People in Texas and Mexico listened to musicians from both sides of the river who often shared the stage, particularly at Rio Grande Valley events, further encouraging continual musical exchange between styles.

THE *CORRIDO* IN *NORTEÑA* MUSIC

Corridos are descriptive ballads about the deeds of celebrated people, local heroes, or historical occasions. The genre developed from the earlier Spanish *romance*, a similar type of song brought by the Spaniards to the New Spain (Mexico) after the conquest. Since the 19th century, *corridistas* (*corrido* singers) were considered storytellers disseminating news from town to town and informing people of events in remote places. *Corridos* exploded during the Mexican revolution by informing people in remote villages about political events sweeping the country and familiarizing them with the main actors of the armed struggle. In the 20th-century post-revolution urbanization of modern life, *corridos* increasingly became the musical vehicle of rural people, celebrating the deeds of people who, like them, were increasingly separated from the Mexican mainstream. Thus, it is common to find *corridos* celebrating outlaws as rebels against what people felt was a growingly authoritarian and marginalizing social structure. This is particularly clear in the tradition of *corridos* from the border that reflect the experience of marginalization and discrimination of Mexican people living on both sides of the Rio Grande. "El corrido de Gregorio Cortez" or "El corrido de Juan Cortina" are good examples of the thin line between heroism and illegality, notions defined by specific social and historical agendas, and depending on ideological or cultural background, Gregorio Cortez and Juan Cortina could be both criminals and/or heroes.

ACTIVITY 5.2.   *Search the Internet for a version of "El corrido de Juan Cortina." With the help of your class instructor analyze the lyrics and contrast them to how Juan Nepomuceno Cortina is portrayed in U.S. history. How can his story support different mythologies in which he could be either a hero or a villain?*

Corridos are sung in *polca* style (*oom-pah oom-pah*) or *vals/ranchera* style (*oom-pah-pah*) to simple and periodic melodic lines over conventional, uncomplicated harmonic structures that usually alternate either I-V-I or I-IV-V-I chord sequences. Lyrics are emphasized over musical variety; thus contrafacta is a common technique for writing *corridos*, relying on composing new lyrics to older melodies so that many songs resemble each other. The version of "Máquina 501" (Train 501) included in the CD (track 5) set is a good example of *corrido norteño* in *vals/ranchera* style. A detailed analysis of "Máquina 501" is on the companion website.

"Máquina 501" shows some roles *corridos* have had in the construction of memory and development of popular mythology. Many believe *corridos* to be true stories, but often their composers embellish them to better convey the ideas they wish to express. As a story, "Máquina 501" is marred by minor inaccuracies: the events occurred on a Thursday, not Sunday; the train number was 2, not 501; and most important, the fireman did not want to abandon the train but García ordered him to jump out, a crucial detail because it shows how *corridos* merge fact and fiction by the message they want to send. García is still known throughout northern Mexico as Nacozari's Hero, and November 7 institutionally memorialized his action as National Day of the Railroad Worker; so every November 7 elementary schoolchildren throughout Sonora sing this *corrido* and recite poems written in his honor. At these occasions the *corrido* plays a central role, both descriptive and performative, in constructing and celebrating local events and stories, performing memory and social imaginaries, providing guides on ideal social behavior, and reproducing the community's social values—in this case, heroism, selflessness, bravery, and communal interests before individual ones. Since most *corridos* feature male characters the genre also plays an important role in socially defining standards of masculinity for rural Mexican men. These social roles of the *corrido* are important, especially when its part in the construction of identity stereotypes is explored and other types of (more controversial) *corridos* are analyzed later in the chapter.

ACTIVITY 5.3. *Listen to "Máquina 501" (CD track 5) and read the analysis of the song in the companion website. After identifying the way music and lyrics work together, and after understanding the role of these songs as musical memorials, attempt to compose the lyrics of a corrido that celebrates someone in your community as done in "Máquina 501."*

THE PERFORMANCE OF A *NORTEÑA* IDENTITY

During the 1960s, many *norteño* groups followed Los Alegres de Terán but by this time, the production and marketing of *norteña* music had shifted from the Rio Grande Valley to the city of Monterrey. There, local labels that had initially privileged classical music, jazz, and other popular music genres turned to *norteña* music in attempting to take advantage of the growing Mexican population in the United States (Ragland 2009: 115–116). This shift was accompanied by a national entertainment industry that needed to develop icons of regional identity throughout Mexico. If mariachi had become a symbol of central Mexican identity as representation of the nation in the 1930s and 1940s, and if *son jarocho* had been revived as symbolic of veracruzano identity in the 1950s, *norteña* music was just the kind of localized, increasingly popular cultural manifestation that could be symbolic of its local identity. Groups like Los Relámpagos del Norte, Los Cadetes de Linares, Carlos y José, and Luis y Julián continued the *norteña* duetto tradition popularized by Los Alegres de Terán. Los Relámpagos del Norte, formed in Reynosa by accordionist Ramón Ayala and singer/*bajo sexto* player Cornelio Reyna, caught the attention of Monterrey producers who arranged tours throughout northern Mexico and among Mexican immigrant communities in the United States in the lower Rio Grande region, California, and Chicago. Ragland suggests that the success of Los Relámpagos del Norte among Mexican immigrants in the United States followed the already popular *norteña* style established by Los Alegres de Terán, their willingness to play in smaller villages and rural locations, and Cornelio Reyna's popularity and *norteño* image (2009: 118).

The *norteña* persona embodied by Reyna, with his *vaquero* (cowboy) attire, sometimes wearing the traditional *cuera* (a brown leather jacket typical from Tamaulipas State) or long-sleeved square-patterned shirts, but always cowboy boots and Tejano hat, was similar to that of U.S. country musicians and rodeo fans who also carried a stigma of unsophistication, considered sometimes campy and kitsch. This *norteño* persona was developed through music and film, Eulalio "Piporro" González (1921–2003) being fundamental in establishing such a representation. Piporro started his career as a radio actor and comedian in Monterrey, but it was in Mexico City that he got his first break in XEQ's radio soap opera *Ahí viene Martín Corona* (*Martín Corona Is Coming*), along with popular film star Pedro Infante in 1950. The soap opera was so popular it was made into a film the following year. In most of his films, González played the same stage persona called Piporro that overcame the actor's personal identity and cemented the representation of *norteños* in Mexico's popular culture. Piporro wore the cowboy outfit, sang *norteñas*, danced *polcas* (in his own distinctive *taconazo* [heeling] style), and personified a type of *norteña* macho masculinity that challenged some of the violent stereotypes reinforced through movies like *Los hermanos del Hierro* (*The Del Hierro Brothers*) (1961).

While the mainstream representation of the Mexican north was one of lawless violence and gun fighting cowboys (like the American Wild West), Piporro took that archetype and instilled it with positive values: chivalry, friendliness, honesty, patriotism, loyalty, and good humor. Although a certain macho attitude was always central to his characters, González's comedic vein also provided a critique of the macho violence celebrated in *corridos* and movies. This is particularly evident in his versions of *corridos* like "Lucio Vázquez," which narrates the killing of a man by brothers of a woman he has seduced. At the song's beginning Piporro scornfully intones: "Se murió por hombre…¿quién le manda haber sido tan hombre?" (He died for being a man…who commanded him to be so manly?), implying that what killed Lucio was his adherence to macho archetypes. Piporro's unique stylistic features included jokes and commentaries during instrumental interludes between stanzas; in "Lucio Vázquez," after the verses in which Lucio's mother expresses concern for what may happen to him, Piporro impersonates Lucio's hypothetical answer to her "No se preocupe, 'amá, soy hombre" (Don't worry, mom, I am a man). The overall tone in these commentaries is one of mockery of the type of macho violence celebrated by Mexican popular culture. In "El terror de la frontera" (The Terror of the Border) he ridicules the stereotype of the mysterious manly foreign cowboy who enters a saloon where all the costumers are afraid he will shoot them at the slightest provocation. In Piporro's song the mysterious character pulls out his gun only to offer it as payment for the drinks he has just had. One of Piporro's sarcastic commentaries in the middle of the song ("el valiente le entra al pleito: muere; el cobarde le saca: vive" [brave people pick fights and die; cowards avoid them and live]) is also a waggish critique of the machista value system that praises picking a fight as an example of manly courage. Piporro's personification of *norteño* men in countless films shaped the representation of *norteña* identity for mainstream Mexican audiences as well as the connection between *norteño* identity and *norteña* music. Figure 5.5 shows Piporro during one of his typically comical peformances.

Piporro's performance of a *norteño* persona and the way his songs and screen characters articulated the experience of rural Mexicans was particularly significant since the main market of *norteña* music were farm workers, especially Mexican migrants who lived and worked in the United States. It is no coincidence that the popularization of *norteña* music among rural workers both in Mexico and the United States took

FIGURE 5.5. *Eulalio "Piporro" González in the film* La nave de los monstruos *(1960). (Courtesy of Alejandro L. Madrid)*

place precisely during the years of the Bracero Program when continuous border crossing by these workers also meant the transnational travel of their favorite music. The immigrant experience of those decades is portrayed in the classic film *Espaldas mojadas* (*Wetbacks*) (1953). Here, González, in a rare non-comedic appearance, plays a Mexican migrant living under extreme working conditions for a railroad company. The border crossing experience was a constant in González's career and can be heard in songs like "Chulas fronteras" (Beautiful Borders), "Natalio Reyes Colás," and "Los ojos de Pancha" (Pancha's Eyes).

ACTIVITY 5.4. *Search the Internet for video clips of the songs "Chulas fronteras" and "Natalio Reyes Colás" as featured in the film* El bracero del año. *How does Piporro's performance of immigrant workers relate to American culture? Analyze these songs in the context of the Bracero Program. An in-depth discussion of these songs as well as translations of the lyrics can be found in Cathy Ragland (2011: 360–368).*

While groups like Luis y Julián and Carlos y José continued the duetto tradition into the late 20th century, the continuous lineup changes of Los Cadetes de Linares, with its expansion of the *norteña* music ensemble, foreshadowed the advent of larger *norteña* bands that redefined *norteña* in the 1970s, especially groups like Los Tigres del Norte. Having won five Latin Grammy Awards and achieved sales of over 32 million records, Los Tigres del Norte are the most popular and successful *norteña* band ever. Their music and recording output spans the smaller and more localized *norteña* market of the 1960s and the transnational *norteña* boom that took over the Mexican music industry and expanded the genre's influence to South America from the 1990s.

Los Tigres del Norte was founded by the Hernández brothers and cousins (Jorge, Hernán, Freddy, and Raúl) from the northwestern state of Sinaloa in 1968. Their huge commercial success and continual work across borders exemplifies the type of transnational practice that eventually resulted in the style's acceptance by the mainstream Mexican entertainment industry. In 1974, after moving to the United States, the band recorded "Contrabando y traición" (Contraband and Treason). This *corrido* ignited the band's career, inspired a series of movies based on the song's main characters (Emilio Varela and Camelia "La Texana"), and triggered the boom of the *corrido* sub-genre known as *narcocorrido* (ballads about drug dealings).

Los Tigres del Norte reinvigorated the *norteña* style by introducing electric bass, drum set, and saxophone into the ensemble's lineup; by incorporating musical elements from other styles and traditions, especially *cumbia, bolero, balada, merengue,* and rock; and using special sound effects to support the narrative plot of their *corridos*. They have also collaborated with pop, rock, and *reggaetón* stars such as Juanes, Julieta Venegas, Zach de la Rocha from Rage against the Machine, and Residente from Calle 13. Having experienced discrimination as immigrants themselves, the band members have made part of their mission to support the political cause of undocumented migrant workers in the United States. Songs like "Vivan los mojados" (Long Live the Wetbacks), "Jaula de oro" (Golden Cage), "Tres veces mojado" (Three Times Wetback), and "Somos más americanos" are very critical of the hypocritical dynamics of U.S. immigration laws. They argue that while the United States economy generates a demand for cheap Mexican labor its immigration policies make it impossible for them to enter the country with the necessary documents and authorization that would prevent their exploitation, a situation compounded by xenophobic politicians who make them into scapegoats. The *corridos* and songs by Los Tigres del Norte promote a sense of pride in the immigrants' cultural background and emphasize that they are in fact central to the U.S. economic and cultural fabric. Part of the band's success comes from their unconditional solidarity with the people they sing for and about.

The influence of Los Tigres del Norte was strong not only in the music market but also in the performing style shift from the austere stage presence of early acts like Los Alegres de Terán to the grand shows of Los Tucanes de Tijuana and Bronco. As mentioned, Los Tigres del Norte were also fundamental in the popularization of the *narcocorrido*, a sub-genre shared with banda music, one of the other musical traditions from northern Mexico that became big in the 1990s under the rubric Mexican Regional Music or *Onda Grupera*. Before discussing *narcocorridos* and their unquestionable importance in contemporary Mexico, I will examine the trajectory of banda as a music style that came to represent a northwestern Mexican identity.

ACTIVITY 5.5. *In order to learn more about how norteña music performance styles have influenced recent migrant groups from Southern Mexico in the United States, listen to the fourth installment of Squeezebox Stories produced by Julie Caine and Marié Abe (http://squeezeboxstories.com/stories/story-four-migration/). Discuss it in class.*

CHAPTER 6

Banda Music: From Village Brass Music to *Narcocorridos*

Once, when I was a kid living in Reynosa, Tamaulipas, I entered a record store in search of a present for my grandfather's birthday. Knowing of his passion for the legendary Mexican revolutionary Francisco Villa, I wanted to buy him a record with some of the most famous *corridos* about Villa. I finally decided on a recording of Antonio Aguilar singing *corridos villistas* in *banda* style. I was sure my grandfather would love to hear these sung by Aguilar, one of Mexico's most famous actors/singers. I was wrong. A few years later I remember going over my grandfather's record collection only to find that he had never even opened the LP. Later I realized what the problem was. My grandfather was very proud of being a *norteño* from the northeast and his preference for *norteño* music was a statement of that. He had no place for *banda*, the music from the Mexican northwest —not even if the songs were *corridos* about his beloved Francisco Villa. As a *norteño* kid in the 1970s I was aware of *norteño* music, it was part of the soundtrack of my everyday life even if I preferred to hear *baladas*, U.S. rock, and classical music. But after that day it became quite clear that *norteña* and *banda* musics were not the same thing, even if the repertory was the same or if the artists dressed similarly. Just like *norteña* music was a symbol of the Mexican northeast, *banda* music was an identity marker for the people from the Mexican northwest; and as my grandfather's actions made it clear, one should never confuse one with the other.

THE *BANDA* CRAZE

In 1995, California witnessed two important cultural and social phenomena, the approval of Proposition 187 and the *tecnobanda* craze that made the Mexican *banda* music tradition highly visible. Both events were responses to a larger demographic trend, the growing presence of the Latino—particularly Mexican—population in the United States. Proposition 187 was seen by many as a fearful reaction toward the increasing number of both documented and undocumented Latinos in California, the *tecnobanda* craze was an assertion of ethnicity by Mexicans and Mexican Americans who faced discrimination and racism in the United States, as Helena Simonett has argued (2001a: 80), and an example of the transnational musical flows already reshaping the 1990s Mexican entertainment industry.

ACTIVITY 6.1. *Prepare class presentations about Proposition 187 and the myths about undocumented workers that informed it. Find information about the annual amounts that these workers contribute in taxes and social security to the economy. Comment on the restrictions that actually make undocumented workers ineligible to apply for welfare and other types of governmental benefits regardless of what anti-immigrant rhetoric argues.*

Tecnobanda, a modernized version of *banda*, Sinaloan, and northwestern Mexico's traditional brass music, was created in mid-1980s Guadalajara, western Mexico's largest city. Influenced by the *Onda Grupera* movement and its smaller ensemble formats, *tecnobanda* included synthesizer and electric bass instead of the tuba and horns of traditional *bandas*, added a vocalist, and expanded its offerings by including *música tropical* (*cumbias* and salsa) repertory (Simonett 2001: 29). After the local and regional success of Vaquero's Musical, Banda El Mexicano, Banda Machos, Banda R-15, and Banda Maguey in the late 1980s, the new style migrated north of the Mexican border. Its music and dances (*baile del caballito* [Little Horse's Dance], *quebradita* [Little Break], etc.) ignited an unprecedented craze among Mexicans, Mexican Americans, and Central Americans in Los Angeles first and in the mid-1990s the American Southwest during the anti-immigration moment institutionalized in Proposition 187. After its success in the United States, the style returned to Mexico and with *norteña, cumbia* and *balada grupera*, and traditional *banda*, dominated the Mexican music industry.

A HISTORY OF *BANDA* MUSIC

Many people in central Mexico erroneously consider northern Mexicans a homogenous culture; however, different northern regions therein have their local identity markers. Throughout the 20th century, *norteña* music became an indicator of northeastern Mexican identity while *banda* music symbolized northwestern Mexican identity, and neither was to be confused with the other even though the performed musical genres were often the same—in many cases, the same *corridos* or songs. Traditional *banda* music and founding bands such as Banda El Recodo or Banda El Limón originated in the northwestern Mexican state of Sinaloa although the tradition has extended throughout Zacatecas, Nayarit, Durango, and Sonora.

Banda music's origins date to military bands in villages throughout 19th-century Mexico, but it was only after the 1910 revolution that a uniquely Sinaloan *banda* style began to take shape. Its main stylistic features were its standardized ensemble lineup, which included three clarinets, two trumpets, two trombones with valves, two *charchetas* (sax horns), *bajo de pecho* (upright-bell tuba), *tarola* (snare drum), and a *tambora* (double-headed drum), the prominence of which still causes many people to call this tradition "tambora music." Its core repertory was also defined at the time (*sones, valses, polcas,* and marches) although, like *norteña* music, *banda* remained flexible, incorporating fashionable genres to accommodate their audiences' changing musical taste. Helena Simonett argues that the so-called *sabor sinaloense* (Sinaloan flavor) arose from the timbric possibilities between wind and brass instruments, between tutti and front-line instruments (trumpets, trombones, and clarinets), virtuosic tuba counterpoints, and continuous improvisation of counter-melodic material by clarinets and trombones (2001b: 6–7). Originally, traditional *banda* music was purely instrumental but in the 1960s vocalists were incorporated as famous bands like El Recodo became part of larger touring troupes along with some of the most popular singers/actors of the time. However, this practice did not become a fixed feature of *banda* music until *tecnobanda* in the 1980s. Despite its *sabor sinaloense, banda* playing was not a homogenous style even within Sinaloa in its earliest form. Bands from Culiacán, in central Sinaloa, generally had musicians with a certain degree of formal musical training and developed a more refined style that privileged syncopation. Bands from Mazatlán, in southern Sinaloa, were formed by less-trained musicians and their style was deemed unsophisticated and *ranchero* (folkish). Regardless of the differences, *banda* players rarely learned their parts through music notation, and both Culiacán and Mazatlán musicians continue to learn their repertory by ear (Simonett 2001b: 6).

In 1952, Los Guamuchileños de Culiacán was the first *banda* from Sinaloa to record in Mexico City; the occasion was the visit to Mexico

City of a Sinaloan politician who wanted to promote his candidacy for the country's presidency. Until then, central Mexicans had shown little interest in the loud, rowdy, unsophisticated music from Sinaloa. In the accompanying CD (track 6) you can hear their recording of "El sinaloense" (The Sinaloan), one of the most typical pieces of the *banda* repertory, made at a second recording session in Sinaloa. The piece features all of the characteristics of the traditional Sinaloan *banda* style; it is loud, energetic, virtuosic, and full of the rhythmic drive that made it a favorite in Los Guamuchileños' home state. (A detailed analysis of "El sinaloense" can be found in the companion website.) However, it was not Los Guamuchileños but Banda El Recodo from Mazatlán that ignited interest in *banda* music by securing more permanent contracts with labels in central Mexico in 1954. Banda El Recodo became the quintessential *banda* music ensemble (still touring worldwide today), and its *mazatleco* (from Mazatlán) style dominated the *banda* tradition after the 1960s.

ACTIVITY 6.2. *Listen to the recording of "El sinaloense" (CD track 6) while following the analytical chart provided in the companion website. Read the analysis of the song also in the website and discuss the details in class.*

The history of Banda El Recodo is seen in its many stylistic musical changes and its transnational success. By the late 1950s, it toured as part of the historical Caravana Corona, a traveling company that included some of the time's most popular actors/singers and musicians, including Pedro Infante, Lola Beltrán, and José Alfredo Jiménez. The band soon became a regular at Mexico City's famous Teatro Blanquita, devoted to popular music and political satire, which led to contracts at Los Angeles' Million Dollar Theater. Although its repertoire was rooted in traditional *valses*, *sones*, and *polcas*, it incorporated newer genres like *boleros*, *mambos*, *danzones*, *guarachas*, and swing in an attempt to appeal to its new middle- and upper-class urban audiences and to solidify its presence in Mexico City's music industry. These changes invited criticism from more regional *banda* musicians who accused Banda El Recodo of not being true to the Sinaloan *banda* tradition. However, El Recodo's international success made their performance practice—incorporating some of the style of dress that *norteño* bands like Los Tigres del Norte started to use in the 1980s, and their innovations to the tradition—the

FIGURE. 6.1.   *Banda El Recodo from the videoclip of the song "Te presumo" (2008). (Courtesy of Alejandro L. Madrid)*

model for most commercial *bandas*. Nonetheless, it was not until the 1990s that the amazing resurgence of *banda* was generated by the increasing economic power of Mexican immigrant communities in the United States. The boom of *tecnobanda* in the mid-1990s was crucial for the whole *banda* tradition to move to center stage in the post-NAFTA Mexican entertainment industry. Figure 6.1 shows a screen capture from a video of Banda El Recodo.

BANDA AFTER NAFTA. THE TRANSNATIONAL RE-IMAGINATION OF *BANDA* MUSIC

Tecnobanda, quebradita, and *música durangunese* (Music from Durango) are interrelated sub-genres of the *banda* music tradition that developed or were popularized in Mexican American communities in the United States before they were fully embraced by audiences in Mexico. These styles are witnesses to a formidable post-NAFTA cultural shift that changed Mexico economically and culturally. These musics account for how Mexican American culture, traditionally neglected and marginalized in discourses of *mexicanidad* (Mexicaness/Mexican identity), became central to its 21st-century re-conceptualization. In the mid-1990s, *tecnobanda* groups like Banda Machos, Banda Maguey, and Banda R-15 helped revitalize the tradition by modernizing the ensemble's lineup, incorporating fast rhythms, elaborate *vaquero* outfits, and choreographies that established a strong performance connection between the musicians on stage and the audience on the dance floor, dancing being central to the *tecnobanda* revival.

Among the many dancing styles trendy with youthful Mexicans and Mexican Americans at the time, *quebradita* is probably the most lasting and influential. *Quebradita* combines elements from *cumbia*, country-western, flamenco, Brazilian *lambada*, and rock 'n' roll into a virtuosic, fast-paced dance characterized by the proximity of the partners' bodies—often the dancers' legs are in between each other's–and the bending backward of the female dancer as her partner carries her body down, parallel to the floor. Sydney Hutchinson argues that, musically, *quebradita* is a combination of the *banda* performing style with the *cumbia* genre (2008: 35). The result is a brassy and accelerated *cumbia*, the perfect musical metaphor of the type of hybrid genres that developed out of the contact of *norteña, banda,* and *cumbia. Quebradita* could be the quintessential *Onda Grupera* music and dance style and although it is difficult to determine precisely where and how the *quebradita* craze started, it was the success of *tecnobanda* in California and later the American Southwest that triggered the dance phenomenon. As Helena Simonett suggests, *quebradita* was not only a dance that accompanied the *tecnobanda* craze but also what made it popular in California and elsewhere (2001: 53). *Quebradita* lessons as well as *quebradita* teaching videos and dance competitions were offered in most cities with large Mexican communities in the American Southwest. Figure 6.2 shows two couples rehearsing *quebradita.*

Quebradita's success drew criticism, especially from conservative sectors for whom the new dance, with the proximity of the dancers' bodies and the sexual overtones of their steps, was vulgar and immoral. Others believed that *quebradita* and *quebradita* dancers ridiculed *norteña* customs and lacked respect for more established *norteña* music traditions (Simonett 2001: 59). While for some critics the new style was neither original nor "authentic" Mexican culture, younger generations adopted *quebradita* without much questioning. Its success and popularization first happened in the United States, so it could be argued to be the first Mexican American dance style to be fully adopted in Mexico, thus bringing together Mexicans and Mexican Americans in the development of a symbol of modern Mexican culture based on the transformation of folk and ranchero styles into a cosmopolitan space. Interestingly, Hutchinson notes that it was only the second and third

FIGURE 6.2. *Dancers rehearsing a* quebradita *choreography.* *(Courtesy of Alejandro L. Madrid)*

generation of *quebradita* dancers well into the 2000s who questioned the dance's authenticity. It was Mexicans in Mexico who criticized the Mexican American *quebradita* style for not being "Mexican enough," or claiming that Mexican Americans could not do it as well as they. Then, unforeseen, Mexican *quebradita* dancers appropriated the tradition as Mexican and developed new discourses of authenticity about it that allowed them to gain new cultural capital (Hutchinson 2011: 48–51).

ACTIVITY 6.3. *As explained in the text, the development of quebradita was influenced by many musical genres; one of them was cumbia. As part of a larger class project, organize a debate with your classmates about cumbia, its presence in Mexico and the United States, and its place within the so-called Onda Grupera or Regional Music label.*

If 1990s *quebradita* was one of the first clear examples of Mexicans adopting Mexican American expressive culture as Mexican, *pasito duranguense* (Little Step from Durango) in the 2000s shows how these new transnational dynamics have become increasingly determinant in shaping local music traditions in Mexico. *Música duranguense* is an outgrowth of the *quebradita* trend that became popular in Chicago in the early 2000s, its style so localized in the minds of Mexican American fans that they call it the Chicago Sound. A sub-style of *banda* music, *duraguense* also achieved popularity from the dance craze *pasito duranguense* developed around it. Despite its name, *duranguense* takes few elements from any specific Durango (state in northern Mexico) music, instead reflecting the diverse ethnicities that coexist in Mexican Chicago, with styles such as *son calentano* from Michoacán, mariachi from Jalisco, and music from Durango to a base of *tambora* (drum) and synthesized brass, saxophone, flute, and accordion. As in *banda* and *norteña* traditions, *duranguense* musicians play *polca* and *vals* rhythms, although often at faster tempi, covers of older *norteña* or *banda* hits, and U.S. country songs by artists like Hank Williams (Hutchinson 2007: 175). The Chicago sound's first recordings were by Patrulla 81 in the 1990s, but it was not popularized until later, by bands like Montez de Durango, K-Paz de la Sierra, Alacranes Musical, and Los Horóscopos de Durango. These bands' fans developed the *duranguense* style, including dancing and clothing. Their standard outfit is a modernized, stylish version of the cowboy style worn by traditional *norteña* and *banda* musicians. Men wear low-heeled cowboy boots, belt buckles featuring scorpions or horses, silk shirts, jeans, and a very distinct cowboy hat often referred to as a "taco hat" (a Tejano hat with its sides bent upward in the shape of a taco shell). Women wear less flamboyant outfits, usually regular dresses or shirt and jeans, and sometimes may wear cowboy boots and cowboy hats. Like *tecnobanda* in the 1990s, *pasito duranguense* was a re-signification of older dancing elements, from northern and southern Mexico, the United States, and the Caribbean, particularly Dominican *merengue*, within the specific milieu of Mexican American Chicago.

The early success of *música* and *pasito duranguense* in Chicago happened partly because Mexican Americans saw it as a space to reconfigure their Mexican identity in a social context often hostile to them. Many musicians who played and sang *duranguense* were second or third generation Mexican Americans whose first language was not Spanish but *música duranguense* gave them the opportunity to reevaluate their ethnic heritage and their parents' language. The music's link to the northern state of Durango and its musical traditions was an audiotopian space for the validation of their identity. Like *tecnobanda* in the 1990s, *música duranguense* returned to Mexico, specifically Durango, where locals embraced it as theirs. Many Mexicans actually believe the music and dance were from Mexican Durango, not Mexican American Chicago.

> **ACTIVITY 6.4.** *With the help of your class instructor, discuss in class the history of Mexican communities in the Midwest, particularly Chicago, and locate the duranguense phenomenon within the larger cultural context of the historical Mexican immigration to the area.*

NARCOCORRIDO: A GENRE COMMON TO THE *NORTEÑA* AND *BANDA* TRADITIONS

On August 8, 2008, the video opera *Únicamente la verdad* (*Only the Truth*), directed by Carmen Helena Téllez and Chía Patiño, was premiered at the Biskirk-Chumley Theater in Bloomington, Indiana, by the Contemporary Vocal Ensemble of Indiana University. Created by Mexican composer Gabriela Ortiz to a libretto and video art by her brother, San Diego-based artist Rubén Ortiz Torres, the opera was based on Camelia "La Texana," the main female character in Los Tigres del Norte's classic *narcocorrido* "Contrabando y traición" (Contraband and Treason) about a drug smuggling couple—Camelia and her lover—and her life in the Mexican popular imagination. The idea for the opera was generated by an article published in the newspaper *Alarma!* stating that the death of a man who had committed suicide in Ciudad Juárez was related to the real Camelia "La Texana"; the note claimed that the character from the song was real and not fictional, as its composer, Angel González, repeatedly explained (Wald 2001: 21). Taking the motto of *Alarma!*, a sensationalist newspaper that claims to publish "*únicamente la verdad*" (only the truth) as point of departure, Ortiz's video opera instead focuses on Camelia "La Texana" as a multilayered myth, a cultural construct whose meaning in the Mexican popular imagination was created in a complex web where fiction, desire, and fact intersect. Exploring the newspaper article, the composer's version of the song's character, and the work of a scholar who has written about the song, Ortiz challenged the notion that there might be a truth to be uncovered about Camelia. The video opera disavows the creation of myth, memory, and truth in the context of a very specific song; the work is a metaphor of how *narcocorridos* are part of larger social and cultural structures that mythologize, both positively and negatively, the narco lifestyle.

Narcocorridos branch from a specific type of Mexican *corrido*, the so-called *corrido norteño* that engages the often contradictory economic, cultural, personal, and social relations that occur at the United States-Mexico border. The *narcocorrido* genre chronicles the incorporation of marginal, dispossessed sectors of the population in Mexico and the United States into the world of drug dealing, its ostentatious and glamorized lifestyle, sometimes condemning and sometimes justifying it and its violent encounters with law enforcement. Early *narcocorridos* were associated with the *norteña* music tradition but made their way into the *banda sinaloense* repertoire in the late 1980s. Likely because the song marked the beginning of the genre's commercial success, Los Tigres del Norte's "Contrabando y traición" became known in popular Mexican imagination as the "first *narcocorrido*." But *corridos* specifically dealing with drugs had existed for decades prior to "Contrabando y traición," and *narcocorridos* were merely an extension of the tradition of *corridos* about contraband smuggling between the United States and Mexico, especially liquor during prohibition, an early example of which, "Los tequileros" (The Tequila Smugglers), dates from the 1920s. Only a few early contraband *corridos*, such as the 1930s "Por morfina y cocaína" (For Morphine and Cocaine), deal with drug smuggling as it was not the most lucrative contraband enterprise. With the increased demand in the United States for drugs, narco-trafficking grew in northern Mexico in the 1970s leading to the creation of numerous drug cartels whose power increased enormously as they established alliances with Mexican political and law enforcement agencies—both local and federal police and the military—as well as legitimate businessmen in Mexico and the United States. Consequently, the contraband *corrido* morphed into the *narcocorrido* as the songs shifted to the deeds of drug dealers, and as drug dealers themselves commissioned these songs to celebrate and immortalize their actions, lifestyles, and sometimes names.

There are many types of *narcocorridos*, some celebrating drug dealers, others presenting their stories as warnings of consequences about entering that lifestyle. Sometimes they are used as markers of commercial territories by the cartels, other times they memorialize dead peasant and farmer victims of both the cartels and the law enforcement agencies fighting them. *Narcocorridos* are descriptive and prescriptive, reporting reasons why people willingly enter the drug business or are unwillingly forced to sell their labor to the drug cartels, recording the deeds and adventures of drug dealers, but also encoding values that allow one to successfully rise in this highly stratified world. For example, "El gallo jugado" (The Experienced Rooster) a *narcocorrido* sung by Los Cuacos del Norte warns newcomers into the narco lifestyle to be careful who they trust "porque hasta el mejor amigo / bien los puede traicionar" (because even your best friend / might as well betray you), while lyrics in "Pacas de a kilo" (Kilo Packs) by Los Tigres del Norte are insider code words (for example, *ganado sin garrapatas* [cattle without ticks] for marijuana without seeds). *Narcocorridos* emphasize codes of honor and loyalty, social hierarchies, and interpersonal relations in the lifestyle of drug trafficking as a fundamentally transnational, subaltern capitalist venture, while other songs tackle political implications.

Besides Los Tigres del Norte, another prominent *narcocorrido* musician in the 1970s and 1980s was Rosalino "Chalino" Sánchez (1960–92), a *banda* singer from Sinaloa credited by some journalists with developing the so-called gangsta persona that came to characterize *narcocorrido* singers. He became famous after a shooting during one of his concerts in California, when he returned fire after a fan shot him. In the late 1970s, Chalino Sánchez illegally crossed the border to work in the California fields. He was quickly discovered, and by the end of the 1980s was very popular among Mexicans and Mexican Americans in California and in northwestern Mexico. His singing style was rough, with a high-pitched, nasal sound, and he cultivated a down-to-earth persona that resonated with the peasant roots of his fans. This translated into a music style that, as Elijah Wald puts it, was direct and had unprecedented gore in the genre (2001: 73). He was also the first *narcocorrido* singer to be pictured with guns on his album covers, a feature that became a signature of the *narcocorrido* singers who followed. In 1992, after a concert in Culiacán, Sinaloa, Chalino was kidnapped and killed under strange circumstances; although nobody was ever charged with his murder, many consider his death the first in a long list of musicians dead due to narco-related violence.

Violence related to drug trafficking in Mexico had been largely under control during the 1970s, 1980s, and 1990s, partly due to unofficial agreements between the cartels and local, state, and presumably federal officials, but the defeat of the PRI, Mexico's ruling party since the 1930s, and a change of political party in 2000 created a power imbalance between the cartels and the government and also among the cartels. What started as a conflict among drug lords for the control of trafficking routes after the 2000 elections became a generalized war when the federal government tried to use the army to ease the problem. The escalation of violence reached a dramatic climax after 2010, with thousands of civilian casualties and many Mexican towns and cities—especially at the border, but also in the countryside—under the control of drug cartels. Now, *narcocorrido* singers associated with specific cartels also became targets of violence; vocalists Sergio Gómez from K-Paz de la Sierra, Fabián Ortega Piñón "El Halcón de la Sierra," Javier Morales from Los Implacables de Nuevo León, Zayda Peña from Zayda y Los Culpables, several members from Tecno Banda Fugaz, Los Padrinos de la Sierra, and Explosión Norteña, among others, have been gunned down arguably due to their links to drug lords. Probably the most famous case is that of Valentín Elizalde "El Gallo de Oro" (The Golden Rooster), a *banda* and *norteña* singer apparently killed for closing a concert in Reynosa, Tamaulipas, in 2006 with the *narcocorrido* "A mis enemigos" (To my Enemies). The song, associated with the Cartel de Sinaloa, daringly states "Ya saben con quien se meten / vengan a rifar su suerte" (You know who you are messing with / come and gamble your life). It was sung in territory controlled by the Cartel del Golfo, and consequently was considered an insult and a provocation.

Since the late 1990s, several state governments (especially in Sinaloa, Chihuahua, Nuevo León, and Michoacán) have criticized *narcocorridos* for offering bad role models for Mexican youth, inciting violence, and apologizing for crime, and they have invited radio stations to "voluntarily" stop programming *narcocorridos*. These censorship measures have been largely informal in order not to violate the right of freedom of expression, although congressmen from the Partido de la Revolución Democrática (PRD), México's leftist party, in 2007 proposed the systematic enforcement of broadcasting laws that would prevent and regulate the diffusion of *narcocorridos*. In 2010, the state government of Sinaloa went further, passing a polemical decree banning the live performance of *narcocorridos* at any public place. Despite these efforts, *narcocorridos* continue to be distributed by alternative and underground channels, U.S. border blasters still play them, and they are distributed by piracy; as a result, *narcocorridos* have become even more popular. The *narcocorrido* and its singer's persona have also been embraced by Mexican Americans to the point that some journalists call it the Latino gangsta rap. Furthermore, the ambiguous grounds upon which censorship agreements between government and radio stations in Mexico have been established have permitted censorship of *corridos* that criticize the government's response to drug violence or corruption and crime in Mexico. A good example is Los Tigres del Norte whose *narcocorridos* "El Gato Félix" (about a journalist murdered in Tijuana arguably by orders of a well-known local politician and businessman), "Las muertas de Juárez"

FIGURE 6.3. *From the animated videoclip "La granja" (2009) by Los Tigres del Norte. (Courtesy of Alejandro L. Madrid)*

(The Death Women from Juárez) (about the thousands of women murdered and disappeared in Ciudad Juárez in the last 15 years), or "Crónica de un cambio" (Chronicle of a Change) (a critique of President Vicente Fox's administration), have been banned from radio and television. The most salient case is that of their *corrido* "La granja" (The Farm), a harsh critique of how Partido Acción Nacional (PAN) governments have dealt with the crisis of violence brought by the drug wars (Figure 6.3).

ACTIVITY 6.5. *Discuss in class the attempts to forbid narcocorridos in Mexico. Are narcocorridos an effect of the generalized drug lifestyle as an alternative for many who have been marginalized by the failure of the Mexican state to provide adequate job opportunities? Or do narcocorridos promote the narco lifestyle and attract young men into it? Search the Internet for videos of Los Tigres del Norte's "La granja" or "El general" (The General) to talk about how narcocorridos also discuss current political issues from a critical standpoint. Engage Gabriela Ortiz's critique of myth in* Únicamente la verdad *as a point of departure to ask whether there is one single truth and meaning behind narcocorridos.*

The development of *quebradita* and *pasito duranguense* as well as the increasing success of *narcocorridos* across the U.S.-Mexico border are good examples of the powerful transnational dynamics that inform popular Mexican music today. These music genres and styles, together with their music scenes, have generated a dramatic change in the landscape of Mexican popular music during the last 20 years. Clearly, it is impossible to understand contemporary Mexican music without taking into account the migratory flows that have ultimately changed the country's economic dynamics, including the Mexican music industry.

CHAPTER 7

Rock and *Canto Nuevo*: Alternative Musics in Mexico

The guitar starts playing a sequence in pizzicato style with the cello playing a scratchy but rhythmic accompaniment. Rita Guerrero comes in singing in a high register, doubled by the piano and accompanied by the double bass while a pointillistic saxophone line and drum set establish the eerie atmosphere of the song. At the climax of the introduction the piano plays a dissonant and loud chord that sets the mood for Rita to recite "la existencia es una imperfección" (existence is an imperfection) over an atonal and a-rhythmic improvisation by the saxophone. The decoration of the stage is sober and the illumination dimmed, which contributes to the overall sense of darkness of the moment. This is the type of experimental and uncompromising music that the progressive rock band Santa Sabina is famous for, and what makes it unique in the *rock en español* scene of the late 1990s.

As strange as it may be, this passage belongs to the band's acoustic session for MTV's Unplugged series taped on April 2, 1997 (Figure 7.1). Santa Sabina was only the fourth Mexican band to perform in this series, after Caifanes, La Maldita Vecindad, and Café Tacvba. Due to *Rock en tu Idioma*, a marketing campaign of BMG-Ariola, supported by Televisa, alternative Mexican rock bands, like Santa Sabina had unprecedented access to mass media. Track 7 of the companion CD offers "Canción" (Song), a Santa Sabina song from its 2000 album *Mar adentro en la sangre* (The Sea in the Blood) that sets to music the homonymous poem by Mexican poet Xavier Villaurrutia (1903–50), one of the most important Mexican poets of the post-revolutionary years and a member of a cosmopolitan literary group known as Los Contemporáneos (The Contemporary Ones).

This song is a good example of the aesthetic ideals and the type of experimental rock that defined Santa Sabina's exceptional style. The song is structured in two sections (A and B) that are clearly different in

FIGURE 7.1.   *Santa Sabina during their 1997 MTV Unplugged session. (Courtesy of Alejandro L. Madrid)*

the use of musical material, and a series of brief bridges and interludes (see chart 5 in the companion website). The musical style of "Canción" is rather minimalistic and favors the repetition of small melodic gestures, pitches, harmonic sequences, and bass notes. The main tonal center of the song (E-flat minor) is established through repetition and melodic direction instead of traditional functional tonal practices (there are no dominant chords, no leading tones, and no traditional harmonic sequences throughout the song). The harmony is ambiguous since it is often based on the dissonances between the repeated pitches in the bass (D flat and C natural) and the E flat or B flat centers of the melody. The first clear E-flat minor chord only comes at the beginning of the B section, well over a minute into the song; before that the tonal center is only suggested by the melodic turns although continuously challenged by the dissonant pedals of the bass.

The main melody is made out of the repetition and juxtaposition of five small basic gestures or motives based on similar repeated intervallic material. Motive a (Figure 7.2) is a leap of octave on the fifth degree of the scale that is transformed into motive a' when the octave leap resolves into the third degree (Figure 7.5). Motive b is a repetition of E flat, the main tonal center of the song (Figure 7.3). Motive c and its transformation (motive c′) (Figures 7.4 and 7.6) are the first melodic indications of E-flat minor as a tonal center. In both cases the leading tone is avoided, in Figure 7.4 in order to resolve into the fifth degree (B flat), and in example 10 in order to resolve into a raised fourth degree (a natural). Motives d (Figure 7.7) and e (Figure 7.8) come in the B section of the song and are based on the first pentachord of the E-flat minor scale; in both cases the melody emphasizes E flat as a tonal center through melodic directionality, avoiding the use of dominant chords or leading tones.

FIGURE 7.2.   *Motive "a" from Santa Sabina's "Canción."*

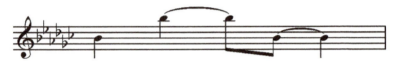

FIGURE 7.3.   *Motive "b" from Santa Sabina's "Canción."*

FIGURE 7.4.   *Motive "c" from Santa Sabina's "Canción."*

FIGURE 7.5.   *Motive "a′" from Santa Sabina's "Canción."*

FIGURE 7.6.   *Motive "c′" from Santa Sabina's "Canción."*

FIGURE 7.7. *Motive "d" from Santa Sabina's "Canción."*

FIGURE 7.8. *Motive "e" from Santa Sabina's "Canción."*

An important feature of the song is the relationship between the poem and the musical material. According to its lyrics, the song could be divided in three parts. The first one, from 0:00 to 1:37, is a salutation in which Silence is invoked to provide advice about the spiritual absence of the loved one. The second part, from 1:48 to 4:44 is an obsessive call for help to a series of elements (wind, water, and heaven) that the poet invokes to no avail. The third part is a recapitulation of the pain that the spiritual absence of the loved one has brought to the poet. The general feeling of hopeless insistence of the second part of the poem is recreated musically with the persistence of the same pitches (E flat or B flat) and interval leaps (octave leaps) in the melody, as well as the obsessive repeated notes in the bass. There are also a few instances of word painting throughout the song, in which musical gestures support specific words from the poem; for example, the echo after "se lo repetía" or the second of complete rest right after the word "silencio" at 4:50.

ACTIVITY 7.1. *Listen to "Canción" in the companion CD (track 7) and follow the chart in the companion website. Identify the issues discussed in the analysis. Discuss them in class.*

Santa Sabina's unique musical style focused on relationships between lyrics and musical motives and structure, innovative harmonies, and use of dissonance and unconventional melodies. These, and the distinctive gothic stage presence I described earlier, made this group exceptional in the Mexican rock scene, attracting a refined, faithful audience that included fans of alternative, non-commercial, and artsy musics like progressive rock, jazz, and even *Nueva Canción* (New Song), interested in originality and refined artistry more than commercial success and media presence. Santa Sabina provides a good vehicle to explore two of the most important alternative Mexican music movements, rock and *Nueva Canción*, and their articulation of a type of countercultural cosmopolitanism different from that of the bourgeois middle classes who embraced the *balada* or the working classes that popularized *norteña*.

BEFORE THE AVÁNDARO FESTIVAL: THE ARRIVAL OF ROCK 'N' ROLL IN MEXICO

Rock 'n' roll arrived in Mexico in the mid-1950s, just another dance fad co-existing with *mambo, cha cha chá, bolero,* and other genres fashionable in Mexican urban nightlife (Paredes and Blanc 2010: 395). However, its appropriation by teenagers and young adults in the late 1950s made it a symbolic challenge to the government's nationalist hegemony and patriarchal conservative Mexican society. An American import, associated with cultural imperialism and rebellion against traditional cultural values, it nonetheless provided access to the cosmopolitan modernity to which middle- and upper-class Mexicans aspired. Conservative fears generated a heated debate against rock 'n' roll and for *buenas costumbres* (proper family and national values) resulting in strict censorship of TV and films while special taxes regulated the import of foreign records. Thus, the style of early Mexican rock 'n' roll bands such as Los Locos del Ritmo, Los Teen Tops, Los Rebeldes del Rock, and Los Camisas Negras from Mexico City sanitized the countercultural aspect of United States rock 'n' roll. Their songs were mostly covers of U.S. bands' songs neutralized in translation in order to pass Mexican censorship. Eric Zolov notes the transformation of the challenge to parental authority and sexual innuendos in songs like Little Richard's "Good Golly Miss Molly" into a celebration of youth and traditional Catholic values in Los Teen Top's Spanish cover "La plaga" (Zolov 2004: 26).

The domestication of rock 'n' roll in Mexico is encapsulated in its adoption by a declining film industry still following marketing strategies that had made singers into film stars since the 1930s. The Mexican film industry co-opted rock 'n' roll in order to replace mariachi music and rural settings in the soundtracks of 1960s moralist movies that reproduced the conservative patriarchal and nationalist values privileged in older genres like *comedia ranchera*. First, these marketing campaigns took the bands' most charismatic figures and billed them as solo singers and actors. Mexican rock 'n' roll stars like Los Teen Tops' Enrique Guzmán, Los Camisas Negras' César Costa, or Angélica María played bland characters, the antithesis of American counterparts like James Dean or early Elvis Presley who personified defiant youth rebelling against conservative 1950s values.

By the early 1960s these Mexican rock 'n' rollers were morphing into crooners and eventually *balada* singers, but the rebellious spirit of early rock 'n' roll among younger Mexicans was kept alive by an underground artistic movement called La Onda Chicana. This movement was part of a larger artistic trend, called La Onda—which included writers like José Agustín, Parménides García Saldaña, and Gustavo Sainz—interested in the U.S. counterculture, especially rock 'n' roll and rock. Musicians associated with La Onda Chicana arrived in Mexico City from northern, mostly border, cities like Tijuana or Reynosa, by the mid-1960s. They brought with them the new British sound that had transformed rock 'n' roll into rock. The sound of groups like Los TJs—and its charismatic, influential leader, guitarist Javier Bátiz—Los Yaki, and Los Rocking Devils, had processed the influence of black musicians like Muddy Waters, B. B King, and Chuck Berry, the Motown sound, and the style of British bands like The Beatles, The Rolling Stones, and The Who, into a new psychedelic sound played by long-haired youth in colorful shirts and jeans. Although some of these bands continued playing Spanish-language covers of American and English songs, most started composing their own songs in English. La Onda Chicana became the vanguard in developing a native Mexican rock movement that tacitly rejected the government's nationalist discourses, especially after its rhetoric was used to excuse the bloody repression of student protesters in Mexico City during the autumn of 1968.

Marking a decisive turn in 20th-century Mexico's history, the summer of 1968 witnessed a series of protests triggered by the incarceration of students after a public fight following a football game between teams from the National University and the National Polytechnic Institute. In the spirit of student protests all over the world, these demonstrations were quickly joined by intellectuals, artists, workers, and professionals who demanded everything from respect of the National University's autonomy, release of political prisoners, democracy, to freedom of speech. The Mexican government finally sent in the army to violently repress a rally at the Plaza de las Tres Culturas in Tlatelolco on October 2 in an attempt to end the protests before the beginning of Mexico City's Olympic Games a few weeks later. The movement, and its military suppression, highlighted the crisis of the post-revolutionary regime, the shortcomings of its democratic practices and its nationalistic discourse, and the symbolic end of the Mexican Miracle, presaging the subsequent collapse of the country's economy the following decade. The arrival of La Onda Chicana and a true native Mexican rock movement coincided with the Mexican regime's crisis, providing their Mexican middle-class fans with a sense of identification beyond the crumbling nationalist discourse of the Mexican state, although eventually falling victim to the political censorship and cultural repression that such crises provoked among governmental institutions.

The Avándaro Rock Festival of September 11, 1971, was the culminating event of the rock scene ignited by La Onda Chicana and the beginning of its end (Figure 7.9). Inspired by Woodstock (1969), the Avándaro festival featured some of the most representative underground Mexican rock bands of the time (including Los Dugs, División del Norte, Three Souls in My Mind, El Ritual, Peace and Love, and Los Yaki) performing in an open field for an audience of more than 150,000. But the presence of naked people, consumption of drugs, large presence of working-class fans—regardless of the organizers' attempt

FIGURE 7.9.   *Fan at the Avándaro Rock Festival from Alfredo Gurrola's documentary* Avándaro *(1971). (Courtesy of Alejandro L. Madrid)*

to draw a middle- and upper-class audience—and suspension of the concert's live radio transmission when singers started cursing, caused trouble. The mainstream media stigmatized the event, reporting it as an orgy of sex, drugs, and crime, while left-wing intellectuals criticized the bands for singing in English and accused the festival of being an extreme example of United States' cultural imperialism. The government of President Luis Echeverría used these attacks by the Mexican right and left to pressure the entertainment industry into censoring rock music. Soon, rock concerts were practically forbidden, contracts cancelled, and Mexican rock music disappeared from radio and TV, further pushing the native rock scene underground. Few bands survived during the 1970s and those that did had to change their strategy, returning to singing in Spanish and developing a new network of performance spaces called *hoyos fonquis* (funky holes) that privileged rhythm and blues, hard rock, and eventually a kind of punk/metal/dark style of music that became particularly popular among gangs in working-class neighborhoods. During those years Mexican rock became a true underground and alternative endeavor that survived due to the passionate effort of its musicians and loyal fan base.

FROM *NUEVA CANCIÓN* TO *CANTO NUEVO*

The post-1968 Mexican alternative music scene articulated the polarized dynamics of the Cold War. Mexican left-wing musicians, identifying rock with U.S. imperialism and seeking a new space to express their dissatisfaction with the Mexican regime, found it in the Latin American cosmopolitanism of *Nueva Canción Latinoamericana* (New Latin American Song). Inspired by the Cuban revolution, this movement attempted to reevaluate local folk musics from all over Latin America within the leftist context of the times. Violeta Parra (Chile), Carlos Puebla (Cuba), Mercedes Sosa (Argentina), and Alfredo Zitarrosa (Uruguay), among many musicians, took neglected traditional rural songs and rhythms from their native countries and developed an international cosmopolitan artistic scene reflecting a new pride in Latin American musics. But an infamous backlash against leftist regimes resulted in the collapse of democracy under the United States' sponsored military dictatorships that emerged in southern Latin America during the 1970s. This caused a strong repercussion on the *Nueva Canción* scene as numerous political refugees from Chile, Argentina, and Uruguay including many *Nueva Canción* musicians, targeted as extremists and Communists by local dictatorships, sought exile in Mexico. By the mid-1970s, with its network of *peñas* (folk music recital venues), its many independent labels, and a cosmopolitan audience comprised of people from all over Latin America, Mexico became a major center of the *Nueva Canción* movement. At the local level, this movement promoted the reevaluation of communitarian musical traditions previously co-opted by the state in *bailes folklóricos*, of which the *son jarocho* renaissance is probably the most salient and successful example.

Singer Oscar Chávez was one of Mexico's *Nueva Canción* pioneers. In the late 1960s he started singing and recording old *corridos* and *romances*, and by the 1970s also included traditional and newly composed *chamamés, milongas, cuecas, cumbias, boleros, zambas,* and *sones* from all over Latin America. Chávez's varied and abundant repertory shows the diversity of interests among *Nueva Canción* fans. "La niña de Guatemala" (The Girl from Guatemala), based on a poem by the late 19th-century Cuban poet José Martí, and "Mundo triste" (Sad World) on a poem by the late 19th-century Mexican poet Manuel M. Flores indicates *Nueva Canción's* interest in promoting and validating itself through classic Latin American literature.

One unique feature of Chávez's style was in his *parodias políticas* (political parodies), a series of recordings in which he uses the old Mexican tradition of contrafacta; thus writing new, politically charged, satirical lyrics reflecting current events to older tunes. In "La casita" (The Little House) he borrows the traditional tune of the same name; but instead of depicting an idyllic countryside house that the song's main character has built for his lover—as in the original song—here the "little house" is in El Pedregal, one of Mexico City's most exclusive neighborhoods. The house and its "jardínes, alberquita y calefacción central" (gardens, swimming pool, and central heating system) were built by a corrupt politician who desires only one more thing, not the presence of his lover as in the original song, but the Ángel de la Independencia (Independence Angel, a public monument on Mexico City's Paseo de la Reforma Avenue) adorning his garden.

ACTIVITY 7.2. *Search the Internet for the traditional as well as Oscar Chávez's versions of "La casita." With the help of a Spanish speaker or translator compare the lyrics of the two songs. Discuss in class the way in which humor acts as a critical weapon in Chávez's version. Can you think of any similar musical parodies among U.S. musicians?*

These sarcastic parodies, criticizing the corruption, ineptitude, and anti-democratic practices of the PRI regime, made Chávez into a very popular alternative singer. The radical leftist Latin American cosmopolitanism that informs *Nueva Canción* is more evident in one of Chávez's lesser known songs, "Historia del hombre muerto" (Story of the Dead Man). Composed by a Mexican in the style of a Cuban *son* and including a poem by Mexican poet Octavio Paz before the last refrain, this song celebrates the idealism of an anonymous *guerrillero* (guerrilla fighter). "Si quieren saber la historia / la historia del hombre muerto / no la busque en las revistas / y sí en sus pensamientos" (if you want to know the story / the story of the dead man / do not look for it in magazines / do [look for it] in his ideas) warns us that the mainstream media hides or misinforms about the true stories and ideals of these fighters. The song transcends national boundaries leaving the identity, ethnic background, and nationality of the *guerrillero* open ("No sé si era Juan / o si era Roberto / si tenía barba / o si él era negro") (I do not know if he was Juan / or if he was Roberto / if he had a beard / or if he was black) to emphasize that his struggle is not of a country but rather against imperial and colonial conditions that have afflicted Latin America.

This sense of cosmopolitan camaraderie, central to *Nueva Canción* and *Canto Nuevo* (New Song, a more sophisticated genre branching out of *Nueva Canción* in the 1970s and 1980s) is also evident in the lyrics of "Vienen cantando" (They Come On Singing), by the Argentine songwriter Nahuel and made popular by the Mexican duo Mexicanto. Carlos Porcel de Peralta "Nahuel," who migrated to Mexico in 1982, took his artistic name from the word for "jaguar" in the language of the Mapuche (a tribe from southwestern Argentina and south-central Chile). The song was included in *En venta* (1987), the first recording by Mexicanto, a Mexican guitar duo formed by Sergio Félix and David Filio, and became one of the group's first hits.

Both Nahuel and David Filio started their musical careers playing for traditional singers from the previous generation. Nahuel had been a guitarist for the Uruguayan singer Alfredo Zitarrosa, one of the icons of *Nueva Canción Latinoamericana* in the 1960s and 1970s, and David Filio was a guitarist for Salvador "Chava" Flores, the famous Mexican songwriter whose songs celebrate Mexico City's urban working-class lifestyle.

"Vienen cantando" (CD track 8) pays homage to that old generation of non-commercial, socially aware singers/songwriters ("Vienen cantando de tiempo atrás") and establishes a connection between their work and the younger generation of *Canto Nuevo* artists. It is both a tribute to traditional singers who inspired contemporary *Canto Nuevo* songwriters ("Vienen cantando a su entender / lo que otras voces les dejó ayer" [They come on singing in their understanding / what voices from the past have inherited them]) and a manifesto of what the movement stands for as an artistic endeavor rooted in social solidarity ("Vienen diciendo '¡no han de pasar!' / los que pretenden sí destruir / lo que tanto costó / un canto para todos" [They come on saying "they will not pass!" / those who want to destroy / which took so much [to create] / a song for everyone]) and change ("Son los que pretenden un nuevo día / los compañeros" [They are those who want a new day, the comrades]). The cry "¡No han de pasar!" is a reference to the traditional battle chant "¡No pasarán!" used during the Spanish civil war and reused by different leftist movements throughout Latin America during the 20th century.

"Vienen cantando" is structured in an AA'BA'B form with an instrumental introduction and interludes after the B section (see chart 6 in the companion website). The introduction and interludes are based on the same repeated harmonic sequence (i) upon which the lead guitar plays virtuosic solo lines. This harmonic/melodic motive (i) reappears also at the end of each presentation of the A section, thus becoming a sort of musical bridge between sections (one could almost interpret it as a musical metaphor of how the song itself bridges between generations of alternative singers). The A section is made out of two phrases, an antecedent (a), which is repeated twice, and a longer consequent (b) that leads back to (i). The B section is a refrain made by two phrases; the first one (c) is based on the harmonic sequence from the introduction (i), while the second one (d) is a repeated motive that leads back into the interlude (i).

The basic harmonic motion emphasizes a movement to the subdominant and the submediant and creates tension by using diminished or augmented chords while avoiding motion to the dominant as much as possible. There are only three dominant chords in the whole song; rationing the use of the second most important chord in standard harmonic practice is a strategy to highlight the moments when it appears. Just as the dominant becomes the goal of harmonic tension right before its resolution to the tonic, its use with the lyrics "un canto para todos," underscores it as the goal of the song, to celebrate a movement of singers who compose songs "for everyone" beyond the channels of mainstream commercial distribution. During a session recorded for the TV show *El Tímpano*, which Mexicanto hosts for the Mexican channel Once

TV, Sergio Félix stated that the song "is dedicated to those singers who are committed, who say the truth without being afraid." The harmonic practices in "Vienen cantando" seem to support it as decidedly a song in honor of alternative, non-commercial, more democratic musical endeavors and practices. This is a very good example of how musicians may use musical elements to support or emphasize a given text.

ACTIVITY 7.3. *Follow the chart provided in the companion website and listen to "Vienen cantando" in the companion CD (track 8). Identify the issues discussed in the analysis.*

Inspired by Cuban *Nueva Trova* singers like Silvio Rodríguez, Pablo Milanés, and Amaury Pérez, the *Nueva Canción* movement morphed into *Canto Nuevo* (New Song) in the 1980s with *peñas* gradually reducing folk singers in their programs and increasingly featuring *cantautores* (songwriters/singers). These singers favored a more modern guitar style, complex harmonies, unconventional melodic turns, and original and highly sophisticated lyrics. They de-emphasized the radical left-wing political rhetoric of their predecessors yet privileged a progressive agenda of personal politics. Their songs argued for equal gender relations, solidarity with the socially and economically dispossessed, and pacifism while maintaining the Latin Americanist cosmopolitan scope of *Nueva Canción*. Singers like Guadalupe Pineda and Eugenia León, and composers like Marcial Alejandro and Pepe Elorza exemplify this shift together with a less radical position against rock, since some of them moved smoothly between the two styles.

One of today's best-known exponents of Mexican *Canto Nuevo* is Mexicanto (Figure 7.10), a duo started in the mid-1980s playing covers of songs by Latin American *Canto Nuevo* composers as well as their own compositions. Their live performances feature a virtuoso guitar-playing style, rich harmonies, and clever vocal textures while their recordings incorporate instrumental arrangements clearly influenced by rock music. The recording of "Vamos cantando," with electric bass, synthesizers, and a percussion section containing congas and electronic drum set besides the usual acoustic guitar duo, shows how the *Canto Nuevo* singers overcame their predecessors' reservations toward rock and made the style important in developing a modern and cosmopolitan sound.

FIGURE 7.10. *Mexicanto in concert. (Courtesy of Alejandro L. Madrid)*

ACTIVITY 7.4. *Compare the music of American folk singers like Bob Dylan and Joan Baez with that of Mexican* Nueva Canción *and* Canto Nuevo *singers like Oscar Chávez and Mexicanto. Keep notes on differences and similarities regarding musical styles, their relation to tradition, and topics treated in their songs.*

ROCK IN THE 1980s: FROM *ROCK RUPESTRE* TO *ROCK EN TU IDIOMA*

Throughout the 1970s bands and fans developed resilient underground rock scenes in many Mexican cities. By the 1980s alternative distribution networks and concert circuits were established, the most influential centers being Mexico City, Guadalajara, and Tijuana. Most bands performed songs in Spanish, incorporating a wide variety of influences, from jazz and classical experimental music to Latin American folklore while keeping an ear open to the latest musics from the United States and Europe.

One of the most emblematic movements in Mexico City's 1980s underground music scene was the so-called *rock rupestre* (rupestrian rock), which combined elements from blues and *Canto Nuevo* in a very specific urban setting. Rodrigo González "Rockdrigo"'s music is a perfect example of the direct, casual, and sardonic style of *rupestre* musicians. Known as El Profeta del Nopal (the Nopal Prophet), Rockdrigo moved to Mexico City from his native Tampico at the end of the 1970s where he started his music career. Embracing the city's culture, he emphasized urban stories filled with idiomatic expressions and *albures* (wordplays with double meaning) from Mexico City's working-class lingo (as in "Rock del ET" [ET's Rock or This Thing's Rock]). His songs range from laments like "Perro en el periférico" (Dog in the Freeway), likening people's disillusions with modern urban life to the feelings of a dog trying to sort its way out of a highway, to sarcastic commentaries like "Balada del asalariado" (Ballad of the Wage-Earner), on how consumerism conditions our emotional life: "vi venir al cartero / me entretuve pensando en una carta de amor / más no, era la cuenta del refri y del televisor" (I saw the mailman coming / and started dreaming of a love letter / but no, they were the bills for the fridge and the television set). Rockdrigo's style reflected influences by Bob Dylan, especially in performances based on solo guitar and harmonica, and *Canto Nuevo* Cuban composer Silvio Rodríguez, as well as an odd yet charming mix of the humor of traditional Mexican songwriters Salvador "Chava" Flores and the pathos of *ranchera* icon José Alfredo Jiménez.

A great example of *rock rupestre* song is Jaime López's famous "Chilanga banda" (Mexico City Gang), which describes the experiences of a taxi driver and uses exclusively a near-impenetrable Mexico City lingo. Typical working-class phrases ("chin chin si me la recuerdan / carcacha y se les retacha") and their intonation wonderfully drive the musicality of the song. A version of this song was recorded by Café Tacvba in the 1990s.

ACTIVITY 7.5. *Search the Internet for both Jaime López's and Café Tacvba's versions of "Chilanga banda." Analyze the lyrics, music, and compare the versions. How are they different? How are they similar? Pay particular attention to how Mexico City's typical speech intonation is used as a musical element. Discuss in class.*

Although not part of the *rupestre* movement, El Personal, a band from Guadalajara heavily influenced by reggae, shares the movement's desire to celebrate the city and an acute sense of humor aimed at their city's conservative values. "La tapatía" (The Girl from Guadalajara) describes the process of falling in love with a girl while walking together through downtown Guadalajara. The song's narrative is filled with humorously ridiculous imagery ("le disparé dos pepinos" [I treated her to two cucumbers]) ("se comió cuatro tostadas, ocho sopes, un pozole" [she ate four tostadas, eight sopes, one pozole]) that sabotages any easy romantic song formulas. More irreverent is El Personal's mocking commentary on repressive sexual values (and a tacit celebration of masturbation) in "Niño, déjese ahí" (Kid Leave Your Thing Alone). The first part of the song lists all the fear-inducing myths about masturbation ("te vas a quedar enano / te van a salir muchos pelos / en la palma de la mano" [you will stay a midget / many hairs will grow / in the palm of your hand]), mingling them with sarcastic and self-mocking remarks like "Que va a venir Margaret Thatcher / Que va a venir El Personal / y se van a poner a tocar, ¡ay ay ay!" [Margaret Thatcher will come / El Personal will come / and they will start playing, ay ay ay!]). The song ends with the singer borrowing the main melody from Dámaso Pérez Prado's classic "Mambo del ruletero" (Taxi Driver Mambo); and using all possible synonyms for "masturbator" in Mexican lingo. With these songs and attitude the *rupestres* and other rock musicians brought a less superficial and more critical approach to rock composition in the early 1980s Mexican scene.

The year 1985 is both a symbolic and real end of an era characterized by contempt for mainstream media and commercial success for Mexican rock. Rockdrigo died in his apartment during that year's earthquake in Mexico City and Three Souls in My Mind, an alternative band still around since the Avándaro festival, morphed into El Tri and released its first LP, its commercial success opening the door to its becoming the icon it is today. The moment of change came when *Rock en tu Idioma* was launched by BMG Ariola with Televisa's support and the TV network for the first time allowed alternative musicians to participate in its sacrosanct OTI Festival. In it, *rupestre* Jaime López sang "no hay peor lucha que la Lucha Villa" (there is no worst struggle [*lucha*] than Lucha Villa), lampooning *ranchera* singer Lucha Villa, one of Televisa's main music stars. López's irreverent take was celebrated by some but despised by others as an insult to an icon of "official" Mexican music. López's song did not go far in the competition but another *rupestre*, Marcial Alejandro, took first place with "El fandango aquí" (The Celebration Is Here) sung by Eugenia León, eventually winning the festival's international edition.

As Mexico's middle class embraced rock in Spanish, the mainstream media discovered its economic potential. This created a moral dilemma for rock musicians who had developed their aura of authenticity partly because they had remained marginal to mainstream media. For many of them, particularly from the older generation, having access to Televisa and the major labels symbolized selling out; but younger bands welcomed this opportunity to distribute their music to a larger audience without compromising their artistic principles. This was the case with bands like Santa Sabina and Maldita Vecindad y los Hijos del Quinto Patio, which remained experimental and challenging as they entered the mainstream media distribution networks. Other bands promoted under the label *Rock en tu Idioma* were blatant commercial ventures and lasted only a few years.

ACTIVITY 7.6. *Female musicians have been visible throughout the history of rock 'n' roll and rock in Mexico. Organize class presentations to focus on the contribution of singers, performers, and composers such as Las Mary Jets, Baby Bátiz, Kenny y Los Eléctricos, Cecilia Toussaint, Flor de Metal, Alejandra Guzmán, Julieta Venegas, Eli Guerra, and others.*

Café Tacvba, from a middle-class suburb northwest of Mexico City, was one of the bands that capitalized on its relationship with *Rock en tu Idioma* by expanding its initially small audience while remaining extremely experimental, innovative, and eclectic. Café Tacvba's diverse musical interests were exemplified in the identity of its vocalist who, early in the band's career, kept changing public persona and physical appearance from recording to recording. Café Tacvba moved beyond the musical and political ideologies separating musics, genres, and styles that characterized older musicians. Acknowledging the wide variety of musics meaningful to a new generation of Mexican audiences *Avalancha de éxitos*, one of their most successful albums, is comprised of covers in which Café Tacvba pays tribute to the *rupestre* and *hoyo fonqui* scenes of the early 1980s ("Chilanga banda" by Jaime López, "Alarma" by Botellita de Jerez), the commercial pop and *balada* of the mainstream entertainment industry ("No controles" previously recorded by the pop female trio Flans [the Mexican response to Bananarama] and Leo Dan's "Cómo te extraño"), *bolero* (Alberto Domínguez's "Perfidia"), and traditional

Mexican *son* (in their *son huasteco* rendition of Juan Luis Guerra's popular bachata "Ojalá que llueva café").

Café Tacvba's new eclecticism greatly influenced the next generation of rock bands; contemporary Mexican bands are no longer ashamed of borrowing from a variety of stylistic sources unlike previous rock musicians who were invested in discourses of authenticity and distinction. El Gran Silencio (which mixes rock with the sound of Monterrey's *cumbia* and *norteña* scenes, ska, and rap), Cartel de Santa (a hip-hop band that unabashedly samples 1970s *balada*), Plastilina Mosh (a duo that combines rock, electronica, rap, and the easy listening sound of Franck Purcell, Percy Faith, and Juan García Esquivel within a retro, kitsch sensitivity), Nortec Collective (with their electronica based on samples from *banda* and *norteña* music) are examples of this new dynamic. New artists crisscross boundaries between styles, genres, and ideologies, and many rock bands have been involved in progressive causes, Santa Sabina's support of the Zapatista movement and its struggle against neoliberalism and for indigenous rights in the southern state of Chiapas being a good example.

I started this book describing a concert by Lila Downs at Chicago's House of Blues, a prime example of the new eclecticism among Mexican musicians. It is difficult to put a label on Lila Downs. Some of her work could be classified as *Canto Nuevo*, but she also performs traditional folk musics as the first generation of *Nueva Canción* singers did; she is not ashamed to celebrate her indigenous background singing *boleros* in Nahuatl or Zapotec; and she has no problem singing *cumbias* or *norteñas* along with hip-hop and Woody Guthrie songs. Her work, her musical persona, and her own personal identity are a wonderful metaphor of how contemporary *mexicanidad* is continually defined by crossing political, cultural, and ethnic boundaries no longer sacrosanct. Lila Downs' authenticity is no longer constructed through her ascription to a pure genre or style; her authenticity comes not from a given or unaltered essence but rather from recognizing and embracing the cultural, ethnic, national, and musical multiplicities within her. There is no better metaphor than Lila and her music to describe the complexity of the contemporary Mexican experience. Music and the social, cultural, political, and cultural processes that make it meaningful in production, consumption, and distribution within and beyond national boundaries, offer a wonderful and unique insight into understanding this complexity.

Glossary

∞

Audiotopia A theoretical concept to understand music as a sonic and social space where contradictory cultural formations (racial and ethnic categories, understandings of citizenship, etc.) enter in contact.

Authenticity A cultural construction that refers to the idea of truthfulness and faithfulness to an original essence.

Balada A recent variant of the *bolero* genre that emerged in the 1960s. It is characterized by a fusion of elements of the "classic" *bolero* of the 1950s with others derived from international pop music.

Bolero A slow-tempo, duple-meter type of romantic song. The style is characterized by extended harmonies and accompaniment by particular rhythms played on the claves, maracas, or other percussion instruments. The Latin American *bolero* developed in late 19th-century Cuba but quickly spread throughout Latin America.

Border Blaster Commercial radio stations that broadcast from one nation to another.

Chilena A Mexican musical genre from the Costa Chica region (Oaxaca and Guerrero). It has its origins in the Chilean *cueca*, which arrived in Mexico in the 19th century with Chilean and Peruvian sailors passing through Mexico on their way to California during the Gold Rush (1848–55).

Chotís (or schottische) Dance in duple meter of European origin. It arrived in Mexico in the 19th century along with the *vals* (waltz) and *polca* (polka).

Cinquillo "Little group of five." A common rhythmic figure found in the Caribbean and circum-Caribbean consisting of five pulses.

Class An analytical category that takes into account groups of people sharing similar social positions as well as certain cultural features.

Clave **rhythm** A constantly repeating figure, usually two measures in length, that serves as the structural basis for the rest of a piece's rhythms and melodies.

Contrafacta The practice of substituting one text by another without changing the melody or harmony of a piece.

Corrido Narrative ballad. Most likely deriving from the Spanish *romance*, in which *copla* after *copla* is sung to a repeated strophic melody to tell an often epic story; the *corrido* in Mexico is historically associated with its apogee during the Mexican Revolution (1910–21). Often referred to as a musical "newspaper," *corridos* recount real and imagined events, memorializing and/or idealizing them in the process. The *corrido*'s popularity continues today, particularly in the repertoire of the accordion-driven *conjunto norteño* "northern style combo," associated with Mexico's northern border region.

Cosmopolitan Worldly. A person who is at ease with different cultures. A type of cultural formation that is widely geographically diffused across different countries but sometimes only involves certain portions of the population of given countries.

Crooner A singer of soft and sentimental popular ballads.

Cultural capital The accumulated cultural knowledge, beyond economic assets, that may allow social mobility and distinction.

Cultural imperialism The imposition of the cultural values of one nation over another. A type of colonialism in which the cultural goods of the Western powers replace local ones in developing countries.

Décima A 10-line, Spanish-derived poetic form prominent in *son jarocho* as well as many Caribbean music traditions.

Diaspora A term used to reference various cultural formations including African-influenced cultures of the Americas. It implies three core elements: the movement or displacement of populations, notions of a shared homeland that displaced groups have left behind, and a degree of boundary maintenance that displaced groups retain in social and cultural terms from others.

Ethnicity A term used to characterize the cultural heritage of minority groups in modern, urban, multicultural societies. Those asserting their ethnicity attempt to reassert cultural difference rather than conform to mainstream behavior.

Fandango A collective celebration involving music, dance, and often improvisation of lyrics.

Gender Cultural construction of maleness and femaleness.

Globalization The process of increasing interdependence between nation-states (through faster flows of capital, goods, information, people, and their culture) and the intensification of a global consciousness.

Hemiola See *sesquiáltera*.

Heteronormativity The social norms and rules that naturalize heterosexual standards as universal.

Homophony "Same voice." Musical texture of block chords, or melody with chords.

Huapango A music and dance tradition of northeastern Mexico's Huasteca region. The dance was traditionally performed on a wooden platform and was accompanied by a regional style of music, with violin and two regional guitars strummed in a distinctive rhythmic fashion. The singing was often ornamented with falsetto breaks.

Ibero-America A geopolitical term that refers collectively to Spain, Portugal, and the countries that were their former colonies in the Americas.

Indigenismo A political project that aims at the development of discourses of national identity based on pre-Columbian indigenous civilizations as symbols and banners of the nation-state. This project was particularly central to Mexican political and cultural life in the 1930s.

Jarana A guitar-shaped fretted instrument strung in five courses. It is used for harmonic and rhythmic accompaniment in *son jarocho* music.

Mariachi In modern times, can reference an individual mariachi musician, a mariachi ensemble, or be an adjective, something identified with either of these, such as "mariachi repertoire." The mariachi ensemble's instrumentation typically includes two to five violins, one or two trumpets, *guitarrón*, *vihuela*, and a six-stringed guitar. A large harp might be included in a large-scale mariachi or in archaic-style groups.

Mestizaje The process of mixing of European, African, and indigenous people or cultures.

Mexican Miracle (or *Desarrollo Estabilizador* [Stabilizing Development]) A period of economic growth between 1940 and 1970. Based on a series of protectionist economic policies and programs implemented by the Mexican state, the Mexican Miracle allowed for the creation of a local industry and a local market while controlling inflation and foreign investment.

Migration The movement of humans from one region to another.

Mixtec (or Mixtecan) A group of indigenous languages spoken by more than half a million people in the Mexican Southwest (the states of Oaxaca, Puebla, and Guerrero).

Modernismo / Modernista A Latin American literary movement inspired by French symbolism and parnassianism that attempted a renovation of artistic languages and ways of expression. Poets like Rubén Darío, Manuel Gutiérrez Nájera, and Leopoldo Lugones are among the most prominent *Modernista* authors.

Movida Española (or *Movida Madrileña*) "Spanish Movement." An underground art movement that took place in Madrid during the political transition after the death of Francisco Franco (1975–late 1980s). *Movida* music bands did not have a homogenous style but rather adopted many of the styles that were neglected by the media mainstream. Bands like Aviador Dro, Alaska y los Pegamoides, Radio Futura, Nacha Pop, as well as filmmaker Pedro Almodóvar, writer Gregorio Morales Villena, and photographer Alberto García-Alix were part of the movement.

NAFTA (North American Free Trade Agreement) Agreement signed by the governments of Canada, Mexico, and the United States with the goal of eliminating barriers of trade and investment among the three countries. Within 15 years of its implementation in 1994, the agreement eliminated all U.S-Mexico tariffs with catastrophic consequences for local and regional businesses in both countries. One of the main criticisms against NAFTA is that the agreement allows for the free flow of products and capital but not of workers.

Nahuatl A group of related indigenous languages spoken by the Nahua people. Currently, nahuatl is spoken by about 1.5 million people in central Mexico (but also in some regions of Central America). It was the common language in the Aztec empire.

Narcocorrido A subgenre of the *corrido* (ballad) tradition that focuses on the stories of drug dealers and their lifestyle.

Nation-state A unit of organization that brings together one or multiple nationalities to form a political union. The term brings together the notions of nation (sociocultural entity) and state (legal entity) into a single concept.

Nueva Canción "New song." A form of socially conscious music that emerged in Latin America and the Hispanic Caribbean in the 1960s. The Mexican version of this trend was called *Canto Nuevo* (New Chant).

Otherness The quality of being other or different. The process of differentiating one's self from others or those who belong to our group from those others who do not belong is a key element in the construction of identity.

Palenque A village of runaway slaves.

Performativity / Performative The capacity of expressive acts (verbal and nonverbal) to intervene in social life and perform or do something as they take place.

Pirekua Musical genre of the *P'urhépecha* people in the southwestern Mexican state of Michoacán. Most *pirekuas* are in 3/4 or 6/8 meters and are sung in the *P'urhépecha* language or a mix of this and Spanish to guitar, bass, *vihuela*, or harp, and violin.

Polca (or polka) A preferred European social dance that reached Mexico in the late 19th century, as many Mexicans still looked to Europe for their cultural models. From the close of the 19th century into the first decades of the 20th century, several Mexican composers wrote original polkas, many of which proved to be enduring.

Polyphony "Multiple voices." Musical texture of two or more melodic parts performed together.

Polyrhythm Musical texture of multiple rhythmic patterns performed simultaneously.

Proposition 187 A 1994 state initiative that attempted to deny undocumented immigrants access to public education, health care, and other social services in the state of California.

Race Social and cultural category that emphasizes phenotypic distinctions between ethnic groups and individuals. It is largely considered a subjective cultural construct that changes according to specific social and cultural circumstances as opposed to a category based on unchanging essential traits.

Ranchera (or *canción ranchera*) The Mexican song tradition that rose to international popularity along with, but not exclusively tied to, the mariachi. Most often it is a simple, two-part song delivered by a soloist (male or female) in an extroverted, emotional manner.

Remittance Money shipment or transfer.

Requinto A small six-string guitar tuned a fourth higher than a standard guitar. It is featured prominently in the trio-style *bolero*, where it provides solos in the songs' introduction and interludes.

Requinto jarocho (or *guitarra de son* or *guitarra jabalina*) A four-string guitar-shaped fretted instrument that provides melodic solos in *son jarocho* music.

Rock 'n' Roll A musical genre that originated in the United States in the 1950s. It combines elements from blues, country, and jazz. The original ensemble features two electric guitars (lead and a rhythm), bass or electric bass, and drum set.

S.B. 1070 An Arizona law that makes it a misdemeanor for an alien to be in the state without carrying the required documentation. The bill also requires law enforcement officers to determine an individual's immigration status when there is "reasonable suspicion" that the individual is an undocumented alien. The bill was signed into law by Governor Jan Brewer in 2010, but its most controversial provisions were blocked by a federal judge.

Sesquiáltera A Spanish-derived rhythmic pattern in which two measures in triple meter are articulated as three measures of duple meter. It is very prominent in a variety of folk music traditions from throughout Latin America.

Son/Sones Mestizo dance and music traditions from the 18th century. They combine Spanish, indigenous, and African music elements. There are many different regional *son* traditions throughout Mexico.

Son jarocho Folk music tradition from the state of Veracruz.

Syncopation In terms of beat, stress between the beats, offbeat; in terms of meter, accenting a beat where stress is not expected.

Tamborileros (or *picota*) A traditional music ensemble from the Mexican northeastern states of Tamaulipas and Nuevo León. It consists of two clarinets and a home-made drum.

Tarima A wooden platfom where dancers take turns dancing and joining the musical performance by producing rhythmic patterns with their footwork.

Timeline A repeated rhythmic pattern and unit for rhythmic organization in many African and African-derived musics.

Transculturation Term for a process of change in cultural encounters.

Transnationalism / Transnational Cultural, economic, and social flows that transcend the borders of the nation-state. Theoretically, a transnational interpretative framework transcends the nation-state as a unit of analysis and identification, taking into account diasporic flows, migration, and the cultural interpretation that characterizes border zones.

Trique Indigenous language spoken by the Trique group of Oaxaca in southwestern Mexico.

Valona A musical genre from the state of Michoacán. It is related to the corrido and follows a 10-line strophe pattern called *décima*.

Vals (or waltz) Dance in triple meter of European origin. It arrived in Mexico in the 19th century along with the schottische and the polka.

Vihuela A guitar-shaped fretted instrument that provides rhythmic and chordal acompaniment for the music played by the mariachi.

Word painting A compositional device or technique in vocal music by which music tries to imitate the emotions and actions described in the text.

Zandunga (or Sandunga) A traditional *son* from the Tehuantepec isthmus in the southwestern state of Oaxaca. Many people consider it the unofficial anthem of Oaxaca.

Zapateo Footwork performed by dancers on a wooden platform (*tarima*). It is an integral part of musical style, providing a percussive accompaniment to many *son* traditions in Mexico.

Zapotec A family of closely related languages spoken by the Zapotec people in the highlands of the southwestern state of Oaxaca.

References

Alonso Bolaños, Marina. 2004. "Mexico's Indigenous Universe." In *Music in Latin America and the Caribbean. An Encyclopedic History, Vol. 1, Performing Beliefs: Indigenous Peoples of South America, Central America, and Mexico*, ed. Malena Kuss. Austin: University of Texas Press, pp. 231–245.

———. 2008. *La "invención" de la música indígena de México*. Buenos Aires: Editorial SB.

Contreras Soto, Eduardo. 2010. "Referencias monográficas para la música popular mexicana." In *La música en México. Panorama del siglo XX*, ed. Aurelio Tello. Mexico City: Fondo Nacional para la Cultura y las Artes, pp. 308–323.

Corona Alcalde, Antonio. 1995. "The Popular Music of Veracruz and the Survival of Instrumental Practices of the Spanish Baroque." *Ars Musica Denver* 7(2): 39–68.

Díaz-Sánchez, Micaela. 2009. (In) Between Nation and Diaspora: Performing Indigenous and African Legacies in Chicana/o and Mexican Cultural Production. PhD Diss., Stanford University.

Dueñas, Pablo. 2005 [1990]. *Bolero. Historia gráfica y documental*. Mexico City: Asociación Mexicana de Estudios Fonográficos.

Estrada, Tere. 2008. *Sirenas al ataque. Historia de las mujeres rockeras mexicanas (1956–2006)*. Mexico City: Océano.

Hayes, Joy Elizabeth. 2000. *Radio Nation. Communication, Popular Culture, and Nationalism in Mexico, 1920–1950*. Tucson: University of Arizona Press.

Henriques, Donald. 2011. "Mariachi Reimaginings: Encounters with Technology, Aesthetics, and Identity." In *Transnational Encounters. Music and Performance at the U.S.-Mexico Border*, ed. Alejandro L. Madrid. New York: Oxford University Press, pp. 85–110.

Hutchinson, Sydney. 2007. *From Quebradita to Duranguense. Dance in Mexican American Youth Culture*. Tucson: University of Arizona Press.

———. 2011. "Breaking Borders / *Quebrando fronteras*. Dancing in the Borderspace." In *Transnational Encounters. Music and Performance at the U.S.-Mexico Border*, ed. Alejandro L. Madrid. New York: Oxford University Press, pp. 41–66.

Kohl S., Randall Ch. 2007. *Ecos de "La bamba". Una historia etnomusicológica del son jarocho de Veracruz, 1946–1959*. Veracruz: Instituto Veracruzano de Cultura.

Loza, Steven. 1992. "From Veracruz to Los Angeles. The Reinterpretation of the *Son Jarocho.*" *Latin American Music Review* 13(2): 179–194.

Macías, Anthony. 2008. *Mexican American Mojo. Popular Music, Dance, and Urban Culture in Los Angeles, 1935–1968.* Durham: Duke University Press.

Madrid, Alejandro L. 2008. *Nor-tec Rifa! Electronic Dance Music from Tijuana to the World.* New York: Oxford University Press.

———. 2009. *Sounds of the Modern Nation. Music, Culture and Ideas in Post-Revolutionary Mexico.* Philadelphia: Temple University Press.

Moore, Robin. 2010. *Music in the Hispanic Caribbean. Experiencing Music, Expressing Culture.* New York: Oxford University Press.

Moreno Rivas, Yolanda. 1989 [1979]. *Historia de la música popular mexicana.* Mexico City: Consejo Nacional para la Cultura y las Artes.

Pacini Hernandez, Deborah. 2010. *Oye como va! Hybridity and Identity in Latino Popular Music.* Philadelphia: Temple University Press.

Paredes Pacho, José Luis, and Enrique Blanc. 2010. "Rock mexicano, breve recuento del siglo XX." In *La música en México. Panorama del siglo XX,* ed. Aurelio Tello. Mexico City: Fondo Nacional para la Cultura y las Artes, pp. 395–485.

Party, Daniel. 2006. Bolero and Balada as the Guilty Pleasures of Latin American Pop. PhD Diss., University of Pennsylvania.

———. 2008. "The Miamization of Latin Ameican Pop Music." In *Postnational Musical Identities. Cultural Production, Distribution and Consumption in a Globalized Scenario,* ed. Ignacio Corona and Alejandro L. Madrid. Lanham, MD: Lexingron Books, pp. 65–80.

Pedelty, Mark. 1999. "The Bolero: The Birth, Life, and Decline of Mexican Modernity." *Latin American Music Review* 20(1): 30–58.

Pérez Montfort, Ricardo. 2003. "Testimonios del son jarocho y del fandango: apuntes y reflexiones sobre el resurgimiento de una tradición regional hacia finales del siglo XX." *Antropología* (66): 81–95.

———. 2007. *Expresiones populares y estereotipos culturales en México. Siglos XIX y XX. Diez ensayos.* Mexico City: CIESAS.

Ragland, Cathy. 2011. "From Pistol-Packing Pelado to Border-Crossing Mojado. El Piporro and the Making of a Mexican Border Space." In *Transnational Encounters. Music and Performance at the U.S.-Mexico Border,* ed. Alejandro L. Madrid. New York: Oxford University Press, pp. 341–372.

———. 2009. *Música Norteña. Mexican Migrants Creating a Nation between Nations.* Philadelphia: Temple University Press.

Saragoza, Alex. 2001. "The Selling of Mexico: Tourism and the State, 1929–1952." In *Fragments of a Golden Age. The Politics of Culture in Mexico since 1940*, ed. Gilbert Joseph, Anne Rubenstein, and Eric Zolov. Durham, NC: Duke University Press, pp. 91–115.

Sheehy, Daniel. 1999. "Popular Mexican Musical Traditions. The *Mariachi* of West Mexico and the *Conjunto Jarocho* of Veracruz." In *Music in Latin American Culture. Regional Traditions*, ed. John M. Schechter. New York: Schirmer Books, pp. 34–79.

———. 2006. *Mariachi Music in America. Experiencing Music. Expressing Culture*, New York: Oxford University Press.

Simonett, Helena. 2001a. *Banda. Mexican Musical Life across Borders.* Middletown, CT: Wesleyan University Press.

———. 2001b. "Bandas sinaloenses. Música tambora." Booklet for *Bandas sinaloenses. Música tambora.* Arhoolie Records 7048.

———. 2008. "Quest for the Local: Building Musical Ties between Mexico and the United States." In *Postnational Musical Identities. Cultural Production, Distribution and Consumption in a Globalized Scenario*, ed. Ignacio Corona and Alejandro L. Madrid. Lanham, MD: Lexingron Books, pp. 119–135.

Vasconcelos, José. 1997 [1925]. *The Cosmic Race: A Bilingual Edition*, trans. Didier T. Jaén. Baltimore, MD: Johns Hopkins University Press.

Velasco García, Jorge H. 2004. *El canto de la tribu. Un ensayo sobre la historia del movimiento alternativo de música popular en México.* Mexico City: Fondo Nacional para la Cultura y las Artes.

Vinson III, Ben, and Bobby Vaughn. 2004. *Afroméxico.* Mexico City: Fondo de Cultura Económica.

Wald, Elijah. 2001. *Narcocorrido. A Journey into the Music of Drugs, Guns, and Guerrillas.* New York: Harper Collins.

Zolov, Eric. 2004. "La Onda Chicana. Mexico's Forgotten Rock Counterculture." In *Rockin' Las Américas. The Global Politics of Rock in Latin/o America*, ed. Deborah Pacini Hernandez, Héctor Fernández L'Hoeste, and Eric Zolov. Pittsburgh: University of Pittsburgh Press, pp. 22–42.

Index

∞